THE
BUSINESS
OF BEING A
WEDDING
PLANNER

How To Build a Lucrative Wedding Planning Business By Designing The Most Incredible Weddings For Your Clients

ANTHONY V. NAVARRO

Copyright © 2014 Anthony Navarro

First Edition

ISBN-13: 978-1497354289

Book Cover & Design by PIXEL eMarketing INC.

The book is dedicated to
Theresa Navarro,
My Wedding Guru

Acknowledgements

First and foremost, I would like to thank my colleagues in the wedding industry…they are my teachers, my experts, my foundation where I have learned how to be the best of what I do by watching them be the best at what they do.

To my clients, for them trusting me to be a part of their wedding day over the past 13 years. To have the honor of being part of one of the most memorable days of their lives.

To my team at Liven It Up Events, for their continued strive to succeed and to be the best at what we do and give exceptional service to all that we serve.

To my family and friends, for your everlasting love and support. For all of those birthday parties, anniversaries and such that I have had to miss over the years because of my dedication to my clients, I thank you for always being there and for your support.

To my immediate family, my three P's, Patrick, Prince and Poptart.

Contents

Introduction

"Why plan weddings?" I pose this question all the time to potential candidates who call and want to be interviewed for either a job or an internship. Why do you want to plan weddings? The answer that I hear more often than not goes something like, *"I think it would be such a fun job. I would love to plan weddings! I would make them fabulous and just how I would want my wedding to be!"*

Well, if that is your answer, you may need to reevaluate why you want to plan weddings. It is not a career path that is about you at all. It is all about the person's wedding you are planning! It is not how you want it to be; it is how your client wants it to be.

I love planning weddings! I started at a young age, when I was in high school. My family owned a restaurant and banquet hall, and I worked there. I really was in what we call "the back of the house" or the kitchen. It was during that time that I remember working with my grandmother, Theresa. She was not only the matriarch of our family but she was the one who really taught me the basics on how to make events come to life. That was some of the best training I have had!

You have the option of starting your career in wedding planning. It is truly an exciting career path. I think what I have enjoyed the most about it is that I get to work with people on one of the most important and monumental days of their lives. I sort of become ingrained in their memory of their day. It is truly an honored to be hired by people to be their wedding planner!

Becoming a wedding planner is a journey, and it can much fun! You will get to meet so many different people from all walks of life. There are so many personalities you will come to find you're your clients to other wedding professionals. I have found some of my closest friends in the industry and would not have met them if this career path was not a part of my journey.

A successful planner is one who does not try to control all of the parts and pieces of a wedding and the wedding planning process. But is rather someone who takes the time to listen to what it is their clients are looking for and to bring on the experts in each of their fields to properly execute and deliver what it is that the client wants.

Try to have fun and enjoy the process. Sometimes you will encounter difficult situations, long hours, and stress. When you can, laugh and enjoy it!

I did my best to write this book so that you can think as though you can work with just about any couple. As states seem to changing their laws, more and more couples are able to get married and will! Remember, you are not just here to work with a couple who is a bride and a groom. You might work with two grooms or two brides. In any case, some of traditions may or may not be used. I have denoted where I can where I think you have to think about how you talk with your couple in creating their wedding day.

This book is just a guide on the key points of how to become a successful wedding planner. I have learned over the years that I learn something new at every wedding. So take it for what it is worth, but beyond reading this book and any others, remember that the way you are going to keep excelling at your career is being aware of what does work and what does not work, every time you work.

Now, let's get you started on a fun new career path!

Chapter 1

Starting a Wedding Planning Business: Ingredients for Success

The Seven Steps to Starting a Wedding Planning Business

#1: Business Plan

I have heard it said over and over that people get held up by not knowing how or not wanting to write a business plan. I was one of those people at one time. I did not think that I had to write a business plan. It was not until I had the privileged to work with some of the best business coaches in building my practice that I realized I needed a business plan. One of those coaches, Linda McCabe, founder of Optimal Level, taught me that you have to have a plan to keep your business moving, changing, and growing. Here is my take on the plan that she helped me lay out.

about the future of your business,
- what it'll look like when mission achieved.

- **Vision:** The first thing you have to start with is something simple. You have to be able to define your business in one or two sentences. This is a one line vision statement of what your business does or is. Once you can sum up what it is that you want to do with your business, you are ready to define your mission.

GOAL

- **Mission:** This is what would be considered your mission statement for your company. What is it that you want your business to accomplish? A mission statement should start with your Vision Statement and, from there, should expand on what your Vision Statement is. This should be about a paragraph long.

what you do and what you will do.

- **Objectives:** List the objectives of what you want your business to achieve. Examples of these would pertain to the following:
  - How many clients that you want to have? *How many weekends would*
  - What type of income you want to generate? *you want*
  - What type of events do you want to work on? *to work?*

- **Strategies:** List the strategies that will help you achieve your objectives. By taking each objective, you can create a strategy to achieve that objective. *Get out there!*

Network

  - To obtain 10 clients a year, I need to meet and book with 50 clients.
  - To maintain a $50,000 income and work with 10 clients a year, each project needs to generate $5,000. Full Service Packages are priced from $5,000–$6,000.
  - Weddings are the only events that I want to work on, so connecting with wedding industry professionals is key.

- **Action Plan:** List the plans that will help you instate the strategies that will get you to obtain your objectives that will fulfill your mission and your vision.
  - Create a solid sales strategy to close business when meeting with a potential client.
  - Create levels of packages that will allow me to charge from $4,500–$5,500 per client.

4

- Get a list of wedding industry professionals and networking events and reach out to them.

#2: Building a Brand (more in notes)

Once you have your Business Plan in place and you clearly understand the vision of your business, you then can start creating what it visually looks like. There are plenty of designers out there who can help you do this. But the things that you will need to build are:

- **Logo:** This has to properly represent the mission of your business. For example, if you want to do formal affairs, your logo should be elegant. If you want to do less formal affairs, your logo should be more casual.

- **Website:** The most important things on your website are going to be:
  - About Section – This is a section about the company and about you. You should have your company's mission statement here as well as a bio on you with your head shot.
  - Packages or Services You Offer – Define the type of services that you want to provide (i.e., Full Service, Day of Coordination, etc.)
  - Gallery or Portfolio – Any photographs of weddings that you planned that you can use in your portfolio should be here. Less is more if there is more quality instead of quantity.
  - Testimonials – Have former clients give testimonials for you and have them there. You may also want those former clients to write their testimonial on Yelp! or Wedding Wire for you.
  - Contact Page – List your phone number, e-mail address, and if you want to keep office hours, list those there too. Having a contact box is nice so potential clients can fill in the information and then have that sent to you. Your website designer can create that template for you.

- **Business Cards:** Your cards should be related to your website and have the same look as it does. Keep it simple, and do not overuse the space on the card. Your cards should have the following included on them:
  1. Logo
  2. Your Name
  3. Your Title
  4. Phone Number
  5. E-mail Address
  6. Website

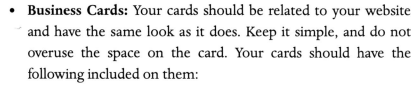

collateral promotional
items:

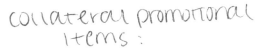

POSTCArds, Flyers,
Packages, etc.

#3: Business End of the Business

There are four business items that you need to consider hiring a professional to help you with:

1. <u>Legal assistance with your contracts.</u> It is a good idea to have a professional legal advisor to assist you with your contracts. Here are a few key points you want to discuss in your contracts with your attorney:
   - Date of the event. If unknown, make sure it states the date will be based on your availability.
   - The scope of planning services you will provide.
   - Payment schedule and dates payments are due.
   - If you will provide another planner if something happens to you.
   - Not responsible for lost or stolen items.
   - All payments must be made to vendors that are third party with you involved in the billing process.
   - Cancellation fees and date changes. Determine what your policy will be.
2. Accounting. Because your business offers a service, that means that you do not charge sales tax; however, you will still have to

pay federal and state tax on your income from the business. You need to keep track of your business expenses and accounts. An easy way to do this is using an electronic program. You need to discuss all of the legalities of setting up your accounting with your accountant.

3. The legalities of setting up the business are something that you have to discuss with your attorney. There are different type of corporations, such as:

- Corporation
- Sole proprietorship
- LLC
- Doing Business As (DBA)

You can work with an accountant or lawyer to decide this when setting up the business. You need to discuss all of the legalities of setting up your business with your lawyer.

4. A bank account for the business is important to make sure that you keep everything separate from your personal finances. Talk to a small, privately-owned bank and see what you can do to get a checking account set up. Create a relationship with your banker. You may want to expand one day, and having that personal relationship with them is helpful.

#4: Creating Packages & Defining Your Client

In starting your business, you have to create packages or levels of service that you will offer your clients. The easiest way to do this is if you offer what we call a Day of Coordination Package; build that and add to it until you get to Full Service Packages. I am outlining three different levels of service that you can offer your clients with services that you will provide. Please remember the pricing will vary per market. An honest way to discover what pricing is fair in your market is to ask other wedding professionals or wedding planners. You would be surprised at how helpful the community is.

Day of Coordination (Price Ranges from $500–$2,000)

- E-mail Support
- Vendor Recommendations

Step in a month before. (Get to know them)

- There will be one meeting to discuss Time Line, Day of Logistics, Family & Wedding Party Information, and Personal Item Check List and to gather Vendor Contact Information.
- There will be a second meeting to do a walk through with caterer and/or venue personnel and the décor company.
- The timeline will be sent to all the vendors the week of the wedding.
- You or an associate will attend the rehearsal.
- Concerning the day of the wedding, determine how long you will be onsite and what you will need to do that day.

Partial Planning (Price Ranges from $2,000–$3,500)

- You will assist in planning three parts of the wedding directly.
- You will help them find a venue.
- Work to get the catering menus and proposal secured.
- Help design the room and work directly with the décor company.
- This includes all Day of Coordination Package & Service items.

Full Service Event Planning (Price Ranges from $3,500–$6,000)

- Manage vendor relations for ceremony and reception and act as a liaison between you and the vendors.
- Advise on *Venue* selection and coordination for ceremony and reception.
- Coordination of the *Catering* selection: gather proposals, develop menus, coordinate tastings, and assist with details
- Assist in *event design* by consulting on color selection, linens, lighting, floral design, and accents.

- Consult on **cake** design and flavors or dessert selections.
- Provide a list of **music** options for ceremony and reception.
- Refer **photographers**, **videographers**, **photo-booth**, and **audio visual production** for your event.
- Help to coordinate **invitations** and save-the-date cards.
- Provide a list of professional **make-up** and **hairstyling artists**.
- Assist with guest accommodations at **hotels**.
- Coordinate the **transportation** logistics
- Coordinate the **rehearsal dinner** and the **day after brunch**.
- Create floor plans and layouts for your event.
- Final site visit/ walk through
- Design processional and recessional for ceremony.
- Provide security options for your event.
- Manage permits, licensing, and insurance.
- All Day of Coordination Duties as well

Defining Your Client

One of the most important part of owning a business and taking what you are most passionate about and making it your life's work, you have to enjoy who you work with. If you want to design and plan traditional, ballroom weddings, then you have to be relatable and want to attract traditional couples. If you want to plan more modern weddings in a unique or unusual setting, you have to attract the more modern or urban couple. You also have to remember, that not every couple you are going to work with will be a bride and a groom. You may want to work with two grooms or two brides. I am all about the love, and work with any couple!

List the qualities that you would like to see in your client.

1. Easy going.
2. Traditional

9

3. Decisive

4.

5.

6.

Having a good relationship with your clients is just as important as having a good relationship with your vendors. There has to be a level of trust between both parties, and you both have to want to work with one another. Listen to the little voice inside you when you meet with a client. If you have a funny feeling that you might not be the best fit for that client's needs, you should be honest and say, "I might not be the best fit for you!" If it is a love fest, book them on the spot!

#5: Sales Strategy

In preparing for meeting with a potential client, you have to begin to think about how you will handle the sales call. Here are some ways for you to think through how you will handle potential business.

First, outreach from a potential client. If the client calls your office directly, you should be asking certain questions:

- Date of the wedding
- Locations (All in one place or different locations? This is important for how you discuss day of duties.)
- An estimate in how the day will go and how many hours the wedding will be
- Number of guests
- Find out from them why they want a wedding planner.
- What are the types of services that they are looking for?
- Has a budget been established?

Discuss in some detail your services, how you work, how you can assist them in the planning, and how much you charge. The purpose of all of this is to make sure that they can afford you and that your services are what they are looking for.

Determine if this is a client that you will be able to assist. Also, see how the conversation goes over the phone. Normally, you should be able to read the client over the phone and tell if it will be a good fit. If this sounds like a wedding that you would like to take on, the client seems to be a good fit with you, and it seems that they are comfortable with your services, then set a time to meet them in person.

First Meeting with a Potential Client

There are few things that you need to consider in meeting you client for the first time:

- **Location:** It is common to meet a potential client at a coffee house that is convenient for both parties. Get there early to reserve a table that is away from the barista bar and not close to the music speakers.
- **Materials:** Bring your planning package to refer to and any planning documents that you might use to go over during the meeting. It is also good to have a portfolio of work to show the potential client.

Planning Your Sales Pitch

I have refined my pitch over the years, but in selling, this is the format that I use:

1. *Tell them the format that will follow.* In short, I tell the client I will tell them about me, tell them about the business and philosophy, talk about the service, walk them through some planning documents, talk about their wedding in particular, and then answer any questions.

2. *About Me Pitch.* During this part of the meeting, I give them an overview of my professional career. I hit the key points that qualify me to be their wedding planner. For me, I have had a professional career in events and discuss how I came to the point of wanting to start my own wedding planning business.

3. *About the Business.* This is where I explain I how began my business and our philosophy. This is your story in your own words, the training you received, and how you built your business. You also can explain why you are in the business of planning weddings.

4. *Service of Interest.* This is where I, in my own words, explain the package that I am selling to the client. I start at the beginning and work my way through the entire package all the way through day of duties. In this part of the pitch, I am also using my planning documents and worksheets for them to see and walk through that I use in the process for them to see how organized I am and for them to see that I mean business.

5. *About Them.* I normally do not get too personal at this point, but we do then talk about the wedding. We discuss things such as the ceremony location, whether there will be a first look, the type of venue, and the type of vibe or feeling that they want. With that, I then know how to steer the conversation to again show the client that I understand what they are looking for from a planner.

6. *Answer Questions.* This is the last part, where I ask if they have any questions. Normally, there are few because I cover most of them through the sales pitch, but there sometimes are.

7. *Closing.* I tell them about the financials involved in terms of the schedule of payments and say, "It was really nice to meet you, and I look forward to hearing from you soon." I then shake their hands and get up and walk away from the table. REMEMBER, after the meeting is over, you are still being interviewed. You do not want to say anything to undersell yourself after you sit down with them and you are walking away. A good sales person knows when to be quiet and walk away from the table and let the client make his or her decision.

Follow Up

It is incredibly important that you follow up after the initial phone call, confirming the appointment the day before or the day of with ample notice as well as after the initial meeting. There are so many clients that you can potentially lose if you do not build your follow up skills. There is a rule in my office and also stated in my contract to the client that I will return phone calls and e-mails within a 24 hour time period Monday–Friday, and if they e-mail or call on the weekend, I will return their call or e-mail on Monday. Communication is key, and your potential clients AND current clients need to know that you will be responsive to them when they reach out to you.

I learned this lesson from one of the largest catering companies in Chicago. I first time I met the owner once, I was just starting out, and he said that the key to success in the events business is following up and getting back to your clients in a timely manner. When you meet with a client, industry professional, or someone you exchange business cards with, a follow up e-mail is delightfully accepted and will leave a great impression on the person.

#6: Marketing Your Business

Now that you have the business framework ready and the sales strategy in place, how are you going to get business? You need to market your business and yourself.

Social Networking

If you are one of those people who is against social media, you are going to have to get over it! You need to use social media to promote you and your business. I know that you will say, well, this just adds something else that I have to do to my workload. MAKE IT PART OF YOUR WORK DAY. This is part of marketing your business. In using this as a FREE tool, you will get business from it.

Let's take a look at some sites that you can use:

Facebook – This is a great site for wedding planners. It is an easy way to connect with family, friends, and other wedding vendors in your area as well as sharing photographs of your events. I recommend having a business page and a personal page. On your business page, it really should be all business related items. Here are some ideas on posts:

- What you are working on that day.
- Articles that you read that are related to weddings.
- Photographs of your events.
- Photographs of events that you attend that are wedding related.
- Photographs of people, mentors, or imagery that inspires you.
- Tips on wedding planning.
- Trends for the upcoming wedding season.
- Meetings that you have with other vendors or clients

For your personal page, you want to do the same type of posts, but you can add in some more personal details. Use discretion, especially if you have your clients following you personally as well as colleagues.

Twitter – For this site, I only have a business site. I do have it connected to the business Facebook site so that what I post in Facebook, I post on Twitter. However, I have it set up so that when someone Tweets me or sends a message to me, I receive an e-mail. I then will go on Twitter directly and respond. I also take photos at events and Tweet them directly from my phone as they happen. Remember to use the hashtag (#) and use it to mark what you are talking about. I normally post what I am talking about and then after the post, use the hashtag in front of the words such as #Wedding, #WeddingPlanning, #WeddingPlanner, #ILoveWeddings.

LinkedIn – This is another site that is connected to Facebook business with my updates and posts, not because I target a more professionals rather because it shows me as a professional in my industry. The best thing about LinkedIn is that others can provide a professional reference for you here. Connect with those who you know, and ask them to give you a recommendation.

Never be afraid to ask for anything. I learned from my business coaches that the worst thing that can happen when you ask for something is someone will say no. Nine out of ten times, if you ask for something, such as a reference, they will do it for you!

Pinterest – One of the newest sites, this is a great way to set up albums or, as they call them, boards. You can search photographs of:

- Wedding Ceremonies
- Wedding Receptions
- Cakes
- Cupcakes
- Flowers
- Floral Arrangements
- Food Items
- Inspiration Boards
- Color Palettes
- And more!

This also helps define your taste and will help you connect to your ideal client.

The purpose of having all of these social media links is to create a platform to reach people. I have personally been followed by potential clients on Facebook and Twitter and have received REAL business from it. You need to have a presence on the Internet, and building your social network will help that happen.

Friends & Family – Another EASY way to get the word out that you are in business is by starting with the folks you know. Let everyone know what you are doing. Send out an e-newsletter to your family and friends with links to your website and social media pages and encourage them to comment, "Like," "Follow," or "Connect" to your pages. Get them to talk about you. They are going to be your best cheerleaders. Trust me; they will talk about you and your business! BUT, do not expect them to be your clients. You have to remember, they will help spread the word about what you do, but you should be working on getting your clients.

#7: Networking

What is networking? I think we have so many different interpretations of what you are supposed to do when you network. According to

Miriam–Webster online, the definition of networking is *"the exchange of information or services among individuals, groups, or institutions; specifically: the cultivation of productive relationships for employment or business."* In the definition, we see the true meaning of networking. When you network, you are not looking for business from one professional right away. You are cultivating a relationship. In cultivating that relationship and taking time for the other professional, learning about the other person, and creating trust between you, you develop a referral system that will come into play when you both feel comfortable referring business to one another.

We have all been to those events where there is the "card shark" floating around. He or she does a quick, 30-second introduction, hands you a card, and walks away. They think that just because they have given everyone in the room a card that they are all of a sudden going to get business. THEY ARE WRONG.

The way that I found success in networking was to join small business networking groups. Some of the small businesses networking groups include the following:

- BNI
- LEADS Club
- Le Tip

These types of groups only have one person from one profession in each chapter, and the goal of these is to create business referring relationships with the other members of the groups. You meet once a week, and every person shares about themselves and their business each week. You are encouraged to spend one-on-one time with each other and get to know the other members of the group and what they do. In doing so, when you are out and about at networking groups or talking with others, you then may find an opportunity to share one of your group members' services if you feel like it might be a good lead. By being part of one of these groups, you have a sales and marketing force working for you all the time!

Something that is really great about these networking groups too is that you learn how to write and pitch your 60-second infomercial or elevator pitch. This is a short and simple explanation of what you do that you can say when you are in situations when you have to talk about you and your business. You may have heard this already, but it is really important that you know how to talk about you and your business. Here is an easy, five-step format of how it can go.

ELEVATOR Pitch :

- **Part One – The Introduction:** This is as simple as simple can be. You want to introduce yourself. All you need to do is say your name, your job title, and the name of your business. For example: *"Good morning. My name is Anthony Navarro, founder and senior planning of Liven It Up Events."* No more, no less!

- **Part Two – The Overview of the Services You Offer:** The next part of your pitch is to explain in one line what it is that you do. Do not give too much information but just enough to explain so that they understand what you do. *"We are a full service wedding and event planning company that takes a client's vision and makes it come to life."*

- **Part Three – Tell a Story to Explain What You Do:** Follow up with a story about what you do and how you do it. I normally follow up with a story on something that happened over the weekend. It normally goes something like *"Just this past weekend, I had been working with a couple for almost a year, and when I walked them into their reception room, they said 'Oh my gosh, this is exactly what we wanted!'"* In doing that, you create a real feeling of what you do as well as create validity that establishes you as an expert in your field.

- **Part Four – Ask for Business:** This always seems to be a challenging part of the pitch for people; however, that is really why everyone is a member of the group. You are there to give and get referrals. Remember, do not be afraid to ask for business! This really is an important part of the pitch. You want to specifically talk about the type of clients you want to work with and say something like "a great client for us is someone who is recently engaged, feels slightly overwhelmed, and is looking for assistance in how to make their wedding day memorable and stress free." That tells everyone in the room what type of client you are looking for. What you have to remember here is to specially mention the type of client. In this case, it is someone who is recently engaged, and those in the room will automatically start thinking of anyone they know who is engaged, and if you can show them that you are a pro, they may just give you their contact information that day!

- **Part Five – Your Hook or Tag Line:** Finally, you do not want to keep chatting about who you are and what you do. You want to end on a good note. In my case, I came up with this line that I say. *"Again, my name is Anthony Navarro with Liven It Up Events, and I make people's wedding dreams come to life."* It is a little less boring and reiterates what I do on a positive note!

The other avenues of networking would include joining a local chamber of commerce or local networking groups that are for small business professionals. I always gravitated to groups that were more service based in orientation as I felt that they would be best for me to get to the type of clients that I wanted. Just make sure that you go to the events and attend the breakfast and lunch meetings. This is the only way that people will refer your business.

Networking With the Wedding Industry

You have already networked with small business owners; you also have to network with event industry professionals. There are always events happening in the event world. You can find out about them in local magazines, blogs, or local business social media pages. Get on the catering company, venue, and hotels e-mail lists and get to the events. Start to meet local professionals. It will really help you learn who is who! Again, just like you would in a small business networking group, if you feel like someone is a good fit, for instance, a photographer you meet at a networking event, ask for a business card and make sure you follow up right away and go have coffee with that person and learn about his or her business.

You are going to have to build a portfolio of vendors, and it is so important that they know your name. When they are meeting with a client, they may drop your name, and when you are meeting with a client, you can drop their names. It establishes credibility. I recently was able to book a wedding because of my established name over someone who was just starting. No one has heard of the other person. However, if the other person would have established their name with other vendors, I probably would have lost the wedding. It is just how it is! Keep your name and GOOD reputation out there. It will go a long way.

Blogging – Some look at this as another 'thing' to have to do to promote; however, it is FREE, and you should utilize this revolutionary tool. To be honest with you, I once was anti-blogging. Once I jumped on the wagon, when you search various wedding venues in Chicago, my blog posts come up! It has actually helped us get business! It really is remarkable!

There are two additional reasons to blog. One, it establishes your credibility and expertise in the wedding planning industry. Blog about things that are useful to the brides and show that you know what you are talking about when it comes to wedding planning. The second reason to blog is that it helps increase your website ranking so that you come up more and more when people search the Internet. Again, it is part of the platform that you need to create in order to make yourself known to the public and potential clients.

Review Sites – You will want to set up profiles on sites where clients can review you. Some of these sites include Wedding Wire, which will list you on a slew of other websites, and Yelp! Keep in mind, by doing this, you put out there the possibility of people reviewing you positively and negatively. You do not have to lose sleep over negative reviews if what you do is genuine and you really work hard for your clients to make their experience with you a positive one. You may also get reviews from those who you do not work with, so how you answer the phone, converse in a meeting, or respond to e-mails may all be under scrutiny when it comes to reviewing websites.

The best thing to do to keep your reviews high is to be professional and do your job to the best of your ability and make your clients and potential clients have a good experience or feeling about your services.

Advertising – When I first started, I thought if I would advertise in all of the magazines, I would be flooded with business. For me, it did not work. What it did do as I was starting out was put me at a level where it helped establish my credibility as a company. But now, as a company, we do not advertise; we pride ourselves on using:

- Social Media
- Family & Friend Referrals
- Past Client Referrals
- Small Business Networking
- Networking with Event Industry Personnel
- Blogging
- Review Sites

This is the system that works best for us, and the only reason this works is because we provide quality work and make our clients happy. It is the secret to running a successful small business—making your clients happy and giving them what they ask for!

Now you are ready to get rockin'! Let's take a look at what happens when you land your Rock Star Full Service Client!

The next chapters walk you through the process of how to work with a client on a full service level, beginning with establishing their budget.

Notes

Notes

Chapter 2

Budgeting a Client's Wedding

Budgeting a wedding is one of the most important parts of what you do for your client. This really tells the story on where the wedding will be, what type of food will be served, what types of professionals will be working with you, and so on. Knowing how much money someone is willing to spend on their wedding day will be able to give you the framework for how to plan their wedding.

Create and Network with Wedding Professionals

You have spent time networking with industry professionals, from all levels of hotels to venues, catering, photography, floral, and so on. Having a professional range in pricing is helpful, but understanding how the pricing structure works for each type of vendor is also important. For example, some photographers will charge $2,500 while others will charge $6,000. In your networking efforts, you need to build a range of vendors with a range of costs, quality, and experience. This will help you build a client's budget and give them what they want.

Budget Meeting & Discussing the Vision

This is a sit down meeting between you and your client. You down the list of all of the things that they are looking to have on their wedding day. This normally takes an hour and a half or so, but it is worth it. We are going to go down the list of items with key questions to ask.

Venue

- The type of venue you are looking for: hotel, country club, private venue, museum, banquet hall
- Location of the venue
- Whether the ceremony and reception are at the same site or different venues.
- Will they need to find a church to have the ceremony at?

Caterer/Food Service

[handwritten annotation: Most expensive]

- Lay out typical sequence of events that pertain to food; hors d'oeuvres for cocktail hour, 2 – 3 course meal for dinner, dessert, late night snack

Bakery – The Wedding Cake or Cupcakes

- What type of cake are you thinking of?
- How many layers? 3 – 5 is the typical range.
- Do you want cupcakes instead of a cake?
- Do you want both a wedding cake and cupcakes?
- Do you want something non-traditional, pies, and ice cream bar, a dessert station, chocolate fountain?

Event Design & Florist (Items may not apply to all couples)

- Ceremony Structures. These are items that are used at the front of the ceremony space and may or may not have a religious or

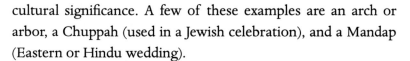

cultural significance. A few of these examples are an arch or arbor, a Chuppah (used in a Jewish celebration), and a Mandap (Eastern or Hindu wedding).

- How many bridesmaids?
- How many groomsmen?
- Parents and grandparents for personal flowers
- Number of guest tables, including head or sweet heart table
- Place card table

Hair Stylist & Make-Up Artist

- How many people for hair and make-up?
- Will they pay for the wedding party to have their hair and make-up done?

Hotel Blocks

- Budgeting their suite in for the night and the night before the wedding and any parents' rooms that they might pay for.

Invitations

- Thinking about all of the items that go with invitations and stationary. There are quite a few. I always go down this list to see what is important to have and what is not important to have.
  - Invitations
  - Reception Cards
  - Response Cards
  - Save the Date
  - Thank You Notes
  - Stamps
  - Programs
  - Calligraphy

- Table Numbers
- Place Cards

Liquor Supplier

- Is this included in the venue or will you BYOB?

Music (Ceremony)

- Will you outsource music for the ceremony, is this included with the church, or will the band or DJ play the music?

Music (Reception)

- Band or DJ? This can be a tough conversation because so many couples would like to have but may not have the budget for. Bands tend to be much more than a deejay, and the couple may not know that. Having that conversation early on is important for them so they understand what the market dictates for their budget.

Officiant

- Will this be someone from the church, or will you have to hire an ordained officiant to marry the couple?

Photo Booth

- This is a fun idea that can substitute favors if the giveaway is a photo strip for the guests.

Photographer

- Probably the most important part of this conversation is to understand what type of photography style are they looking for? Are they looking for more traditional style photography with many posed shots or are they looking for photojournalistic style with candid or non-posed shots.
- Understand how much time they would like to have the photographer with them on the day of the wedding. Photography

packages are normally within hour ranges, starting between 6 - 8 hours.

- How many albums would they like?

Rehearsal Dinner & Day After Brunch

- What type of restaurant or venue are they looking for for these events?
- How many guests?

Rentals

- Will you be outsourcing any items for them? Some of the most common items would include
  - Table Linens and Napkins
  - Chairs or Chair Covers
  - Lounge Furniture
  - Any Rental Equipment Needed NOT Provided by the Caterer.

Transportation

- For the couple: car, limo, bus, or limo bus?
- Will they see each other before or is this a church wedding where you will have to transport the wedding party separately to the church and then together afterwards?
- Do they want transport for their parents?
- How many guests will you have to transport?

Valet

- Will they need valet service at the venue if there is no parking or no parking lot?
- About how many would they think would be driving to the reception and will need valet?

Videographer

- Probably the most important part of this conversation is to understand what type of videography style are they looking for? Are they looking for more traditional style with capturing the series of events on the wedding day or are they looking for cinematic style that makes the wedding look more like a movie.
- Understand how much time they would like to have the videographer with them on the day of the wedding. Video packages are normally within hour ranges, starting between 6 - 8 hours.
- How many DVD's would they like?

Because you have obtained pricing ideas and estimates from other vendors too, you know where the money is going to be delegated. This will help to know beforehand to know who to recommend to them and allow you to be able to put the budget together.

Mock Budget

The next piece of the program is about notes on how to put together a budget for your client. Please note that these budget estimates are based on pricing of wedding vendor ranges in Chicago for the 2013 season. Pricing is subject to change and will vary market to market, but this should give you an idea of how to ask the client and vendors the right questions to get a budget put together.

The first piece we will look at is the ceremony and the items included here.

CEREMONY

Site Fee

- Normally for a church, there is a fee, ranging from $500–$2,000 for the use of the church. For a hotel, there is normally a fee for setup for the ceremony, ranging from a flat rate of $500–$1,000 or a price per person, i.e. $3 per person with a minimum number of guests that are expected.

- Most private venues do not charge for a ceremony fee. If the ceremony is not in a church, the site fee will be included in your venue rental fee (see Reception).

Marriage License

- Check your local county for license fees as the fees range in price. Also, make sure that your couple gets their license in the proper county. It has happened where the couple gets their license in one county and then gets married in another. The marriage will not be valid if they are not married in the proper county.

Officiant's Fee

- Most churches include the minster or priest's fee in the rental of the church. To have an officiant preside over the wedding ceremony, the cost will range from $300–$800. Please note, most charge extra to attend the rehearsal the evening before.

Ceremony Music

- Normally, there is some sort of music included with the church fee. If you outsource musicians to play in a church, they normally will play prelude music for 20–30 minutes as well as the music for the processional and the recessional. The church musicians normally play the usual church songs, or your musicians can play those songs as well. The type of fee for a trio or quartet of strings/ horns runs from $500–$800 depending on how much music they are playing during the service.
- If the wedding is in a venue or hotel, it is normally just the prelude music, the processional songs, and the recessional song, and then they are finished. That would run $400–$600 for a trio or quartet.

Guest Book and Pen/Ring Bearer Pillow/Flower Girl Basket

- These types of items can be purchased from a craft store and will cost about $25–$40 each.

Ceremony Items

- Various items are required for wedding ceremonies. For example, in some Christian ceremonies, a unity candle may be required. This is symbolic, and a typical cost for that at a craft store will be $25 to $40 for the set.

WEDDING CONSULTANT/PLANNER

You have to account for your services and packages in the budget.

STATIONARY

Invitations

- When figuring the guest count, you will have to order about half of the guest count as you typically invite couples and will only need one invite per couple. If you are ordering online or having a stationer do them, you can expect to pay from $6–$20 per invitation. This includes the invitation, the response card, the envelopes, one insert card (tells you where the reception is, hotel accommodations, transportation provided), the response card that the guest sends in, and the envelopes and stamps.

Save the Dates & Thank You Notes

- A way to help save some money here is to have the couples source these from an online source. These will range from $2–$6 each.

Programs & Table Numbers

- These can be made by a stationer, ordered online, or printed at a local print shop. Ranges on these depend on how they are made and are $3–$10 each.

Calligraphy

- For addresses, expect to pay around $4 each and for place cards, $2 each.

Place Cards

- These can be made by a stationer, ordered online, or printed at a local print shop. Ranges on these depend on how they are made and are $1.50 to $3 each.

FLOWERS AND DECOR

Ceremony Site

- Altar arrangements range from $150–$350 each
- Arches: $300
- Religious Structures: $500–$1000
- Aisle runners: $75–$125
- Pew décor: $25–$35 each

Reception Site

- Table arrangements range in price based on flower selections and size.
- Low styles range from $75–$130
- High styles range from $125–$400

Personal Flowers (Items may not apply to all couples)

- Bride's Flowers - Range of $125–$250
- Bridesmaids' Bouquets - Range of $50–$100 each
- Men's Boutonnieres - Range of $10–$15 each
- Mothers/Grandmothers - Wrist corsages range from $20–$35 each.
- Fathers/Grandfathers - Range of $10–$15 each

RECEPTION

Site Fee

Venue rental rates range from $2,500–$10,000 for a Saturday. Check to see weekday and Friday and Sunday rates as they may be less expensive. Also see what equipment (tables, chairs, etc.) are included as that will affect the price per person.

Caterer

Below is an outline of the breakdown per person based on a wedding for 150 guests. This is just an example. You need to consult your local catering companies for more exact numbers. PLEASE NOTE: Catering costs vary per event based on venue, style of service, style of dinner, rentals, linens, chairs, etc. This is just an example of a breakdown. No two catering contracts will ever be the same because the clients' selections will always be different.

- Passed Hors d'oeuvres $10.00
- Seated First Course and Entrée
- Chicken $30.00
- Sirloin Filet $45.00
- Salmon $35.00
- Standard Bar $25.00
- Service Staff $28.00
- Equipment $30.00
- Linen $7.50
- Plus Delivery, Sales Tax & Gratuity Typically, costs range from $100–$150 per person for a seated meal.

Liquor /Beverage

Some of the private venues will allow you to BYOB or bring your own liquor. If so, and you purchase from a liquor store, you are not providing a full bar, just what the client would like, and those prices range from $12–$18 per person. PLUS, some places will accept returns if the liquor is not chilled, open, or the labels damaged.

Rental Items

Normally, the caterer includes all items in their fee.

Cake

Depending on the design, you are looking at $6–$15 per person. The higher cost of wedding cakes comes from the more detailed design. It's the labor cost that increases the price of the cake. Cupcakes – Minis range from $1–$1.50 each, and large range from $3–$5 each.

Lighting and Draping

This section is in addition to floral for items such as lighting and drapery. Lighting cost is between $30–$50 per up light, pin washes are about the same, and drapery is somewhere between $25–$45 per foot. Do not forget to add in labor, delivery, and same day in and out service.

Favors

I typically recommend that these are something edible that will cost between $3 each to $10 each. You should try to accommodate for almost all of the guests, knowing that at the end of the wedding, not everyone will take one whether it is set out at the table setting or at a table after the dinner for the guests to take as they leave.

Music

This will be between a DJ and a band. Roughly, the estimated cost for a DJ in a major market is $1,500. The estimated cost for a 10-piece orchestra is in the $7,000–$10,000 range. This can be a budget breaker for some couples.

Parking and/or Valet Service

You have to check and see what the parking costs (if any) are at the wedding venue. It might be included, they may have the option of hosting the parking and will have to pay a cost per car, or it might be free. For valet service, typically, there is a fee for the service, and either the host can pay per car or the guest will have to pay a charge per car.

PHOTOGRAPHY

This is such a varied service. It really depends, as it does with planners, on the cost of services based on the market, the quality of their service, and their product. I have seen photographers range in price from $2,500–$12,000. This all depends on the market you are in and the types of photographers you partner with. A good idea is to have a range for your clients and see what will be best for them, their liking, and their budget!

VIDEOGRAPHY

What is stated for photographers is the same for videographers.

TRANSPORTATION

Reach out to local transport companies. Some have rate sheets that can explain how they charge. They either do what they call a "one way transfer," where they will pick up at one location and drop off at another location and then be finished, or they can run their services hourly (possibly with a minimum amount of hours depending on the vehicle). Check with your local transport companies for rate sheets.

PHOTOBOOTH

Prices depend on the type of booth and what additional services will be provided. Is the booth an actual booth, or is a pipe and drape booth? Also, will they provide a photo-book that they will keep, are props included, and are there special graphics that will be included? Price ranges from $900–$1,500.

ADDITIONAL ITEMS TO THINK ABOUT

Wedding Attire and Accessories (Items may not apply to all couples)

- Bridal dresses range from $500 to $10,000 and up. You have to get a grasp on this if it is included in the budget because if it is, this will truly affect the overall budget. Also take into consideration in this cost the cost of alterations.

- Headpiece/Accessories, Shoes, and Jewelry – Pricing will vary per couple.

- Hair Stylist and Make-Up Artist

  A hair stylist and/or make-up artist who comes to the hotel or home to get a bride ready will range in price. There will most likely be a cost for a trial and a charge for parking on the day of and for all of the stylists. In a major market, the range would be $100–$250 for a hair stylist for the bride, and the bridesmaids and mothers range from $50–$90 per person.

- Groom's Formal Wear

  The price will vary depending on whether he is renting or buying.

Rings

- Bride's wedding ring: Typically the ring will range from $1,000–$2,500.
- Groom's wedding ring: Typically the ring will range from $500–$1,500.

Gifts

- These are typically for the wedding party members. An appropriate gift range for gifts for the wedding party range from $50–$100 each.

Parties

Check local market restaurants for pricing. Major markets range from $50 to $100 per person.

- Engagement
- Rehearsal Dinner
- Day After Brunch

Evening Accommodations

Check local market for pricing. You should include two nights of costs for the room, plus parking if applicable and a little extra for room service and amenities.

Notes

Client Budgeting
Consider:
- Guest List
- Season (Fall /spring, winter)
- Day & Time
- Region

Notes

Chapter 3

The First and Foremost Piece of the Wedding Planning Process: Selecting a Venue

Reception Venue

The first thing that really needs to be done is to find and secure a reception venue. This is the most important piece to planning a wedding or any event. This will really determine everything else, from the décor, the food, the color scheme, to the type of wedding you will be planning. The space will set the tone and how the rest of the day will come together! The first thing to determine with your client in your initial meetings is the type of venue that they would like for their wedding reception.

Type of Venue

- *Hotel* – Probably one of the most common or traditional venues for weddings are hotels. There are many great reasons to have a wedding in a hotel. Everything is convenient; you can host both the ceremony and the reception at the hotel, and it is all contained. It is easy if you have out of town guests who you will have to consider; if all is happening at a hotel, you will not need transportation. Remember with hotels, though, there are charges for many small items that you have to take into account, and pricing on the menus is never just that price. You will have to add tax and gratuity onto the bill. For example, in Chicago, a hotel might be priced at $135 per person, but you will have to add a service charge (or gratuity) and sales tax. Your $135 per person might go as high as $183.26 per person. That is a large difference, so you need to carefully understand the hotel's policy. Just ask your sales reps! They will be happy to explain that to you.

- *Country Clubs & Banquet Facilities* – Clubs and banquet facilities are really similar in how they operate and how they are priced. Everything is available on site just like at a hotel. The difference here is that pricing might be a little less and you will have to get the guests to and from the venue. Pricing will vary depending on the menu selections, and do not forget to add in the service charge and sales tax.

- *Restaurants* – There are restaurants that do have facilities that can host weddings. This is similar to a club or banquet facility; however, you should make sure that the restaurant is used to serving weddings. If not, you should strongly reconsider a restaurant that is not used to weddings as a preferred location to bring clients. There is a different mentality in working weddings vs. serving a room of people throughout the night on a Saturday.

- *Privately Owned Venue* – Privately owned venues typically are the unique spaces in your area. They are completely different from anything else that is common to a traditional wedding. Types of venues that are Privately Owned are barns, art galleries, photography studios, lofts, warehouses, stores, and so on! They typically will charge a fee to rent the space and then provide some guidelines on bringing in a caterer, rentals, other vendors, and so forth. In the next chapter on food, it is mostly dedicated for you working with a client from a catering point of view. There are some fantastic pros to working with a caterer, but depending on the venue, the costs may increase.

- **If your Client Would Like to get Married in a Church** – Clients must approach the churches on their own to meet with the priest or minister. You will have to coordinate dates, which is really important to make sure that timing will work for the ceremony and for the reception. This can be one of the most difficult parts of the process. Having a great list of church options to give your clients for them to start researching where they would like to get married is key.

Notes

Chapter 4

Planning the Dinner Menu for Your Clients

*I*f food and beverage is onsite at the venue, you select and work with the catering rep to help create a menu that you work with that makes your clients happy! If the venue requires an off premise catering company to come in and serve the guests, you will have to do some work in order to get things the right way! Make sure you find out who is on the list of approved caterers or work with one you have a working relationship with.

Catering Questions to Ask Your Clients & to Tell Your Sales Rep to Get a Proposal

- Number of Guests (Count adults and children)
- Location – What Venue?
- Ceremony On Site or Off Site?
- Start Time of Ceremony and/or Reception and End Time
- Cocktail Hour (Will it be just an hour or longer?)
- What will you need at your cocktail hour?

- Passed Hors D'oeuvres
- Passed Wine & Water
- Open Bar
- Specialty Drinks
- Food Stations

Talk about dinner service with your Clients

First of all, you have to talk about food. What do they want to eat? Are they salad eaters? Would they prefer to start with a soup or a plated appetizer? What type of entrees to they want to serve? How are you serving dinner? See below the four options.

Bride & Groom are served First

- *Plated Dinner* (Number of Courses – Soup/Appetizer, Salad, Entrée, and Dessert): This is where each course is individually put on a plate and served to each guest at every table. Remember, pricing is going to change depending on the type of entrée they select and how many options they are offering. This is because the more options you have, the more team members the caterer needs in the kitchen. You have to determine this if you want to get an accurate quote from the caterer.

- *Family Style*: This is where platters of every course are brought to the table and all of the guests at each table will pass platters around to each other.

- *Buffet*: This is where one or two tables will hold somewhere between four and six items, normally a salad, vegetable, starch, and two proteins are the basic items. There might be more than one of the same station in the room but only four to six food items total. *Better to have on both sides*

- *Food Stations/Cocktail Style*: This is where there are multiple stations with different food items at each station. There might be an Asian themed station with sushi, a noodle dish, etc., then an Italian station with pasta, such as chicken parmesan. This is designed for guests to get up and walk around the space.

Min 3

release call ⚹

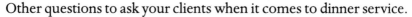
Other questions to ask your clients when it comes to dinner service.

- Would you like wine service with dinner?
- Would you like a champagne toast with dinner?
- How would you like dessert & coffee served? Tableside or at a station(s)?
- Late Night Snack? This is a delicious snack that comes out of the kitchen about 1 hour before the wedding is over or so for the guests to have another bite to eat before leaving.

Standard Rental Needs

- **Place Card Table -** This can be a round table or a rectangular table. It's good to start thinking about this now because you will have to k now when the floral and décor meeting takes place. This typically is a 60" Round or 6' or 8' Table.
- **Gift Table** (6' or 8' Table)
- **Guest Book Table,** same as gift or different table. Maybe use a highboy.
- **Highboy Tables** – These are the pub height tables that you will see the linens that are draped on these tables can be tied towards the top of the base of the table or untied.
- **Cabaret Tables** (These are the same size in diameter as the highboy tables but lower to the ground) and the Chairs

Dinner Service Rentals

- **Sweet Heart Table** (Just for the couple) or **Head Table**
- **Guest Tables** (60" rounds or larger or squares or rectangles. Typically with plated, family style and buffet, there is seating for everyone. With stations, there is seating for half of the guest count.)
- **Chairs** (REMEMBER: These are normally used for the ceremony if the wedding is on site.)
- **Cake Table**

- **Dessert & Coffee Stations**
- **Bar Stations**
- **DJ Table**

Other Items That Catering Handles

- China, Glassware, Flatware, Table Linens, Dinner Napkins, & Fluff Linen (Look at Linen Guide in Chapter 6)
- Coat Check
- Propane Heaters for Outdoor Spaces if it is chilly outside.
- Staff includes servers, bartenders and culinary team.

Bar & Liquor   1 per 75

Below is a standard list of what is included in a bar. Some venues will allow you to bring in your own liquor, others will require the caterer to provide the liquor and some will provide the liquor themselves. If the client brings in their own liquor, Catering should provide the license, the mixers, the ice, and the garnishes, napkins, etc. There will be a charge for this service.

Types of Liquor

- Vodka
- Gin
- Rum
- Tequila
- Whiskey
- Bourbon
- Scotch
- Wines (Bar & Dinner Wine) & Champagne

If you are unsure of how this all works with catering, I would highly recommend spending some time getting to know your catering reps. My best advice is work with the caterer on how to best get a proposal from them for the client to review.

Notes

Food & Beverage minimum:
Hotel - Saturdays $10,000 min (before taxes) to have your wedding there
@ 200 ppl = $20,000 (must pay even if less ppl come)

+ + = tax & service charge (varies)
　　　　 u%　　　　 10-25%
EX: 20,000 + u% + 20%

24,000
+ 1,440
$25,400

F&B and Rental prices change w/ the season

Notes

Keeping the Party Going – Music for the Reception!

Band or DJ?

This seems to be a big dilemma in so many cases when planning a wedding. Should there be a DJ or a band? There are pros and cons to both; however, the largest different is in the pricing. Bands really work well for traditional weddings with a ballroom and sit down plated dinners. DJs work well for more modern weddings with fun food stations. Regardless of what type of wedding you are planning, because either a DJ or a band will work for any type of wedding, what it typically boils down to is budget. If the budget demands a DJ, that is okay! As long as you are working with professionals and the couple has what they want, you are good to go!

You will find below a list of questions that the DJ or band will normally need answers to in order to finalize the terms of booking.

There are some additional questions, such as music selections, that are not important in the booking process but will have to be thought of after hiring.

- Start and End Times? Number of hours the band or the DJ is required?
- Ceremony on site?
- Where exactly is the ceremony room, cocktail area, and reception? Are they in three different areas or rooms? Is the ceremony in the same room as the reception? This is important to know so they have enough sound systems for the wedding.
- Who will provide the ceremony music?
- Ceremony songs normally required:
  - Processional, family and wedding party
  - Processional, bride** (*may not apply to every couple*)
  - Recessional, for the couple and all parties
- Additional ceremony requirements
  - Hand held wireless microphone or a lavaliere microphone
  - Sound system
- Reception songs normally required:
  - Wedding Party Entrance
  - Cake Cutting
  - First Dance
  - Father-Daughter**
  - Mother-Son**

**Please note, these items may or may not apply to the couple you are working with.*

Notes

Chapter 6

Crafting & Creating the Vision for Your Clients – The All Important Décor

The first thing that needs to be done is to determine the look or the vision: something more contemporary or modern or something more traditional, romantic, vintage, or rustic? The best way I have found to talk this through with a bride is to ask for photographs. Seeing what they like and do not like will help with the conversation on how to design a room.

Which direction is your client leaning towards?
- Contemporary or Modern
- Traditional
- Romantic
- Rustic
- Vintage

Decide the color scheme. There is no limit to the amount of colors that are part of designing a wedding. Normally, there are three main colors that are used, and then from there, there can be a burst of color in the flowers that all make sense in the color palette. Remember is working with you client to select the color selections, you have to think of the room you are working in. For example, if the room has an overall red tone in the room, you might want to stay away from green unless you are wanting it to look like Christmas!

What colors do your clients prefer?
- Color #1:
- Color #2:
- Color #3:

In designing, you also, as a planner, have to think of the concept of the space and make it functional. How will the ceremony flow into cocktail hour, into dinner, into dancing? You have to think of the wedding all the way through to make sure that you are designing with purpose and functionality.

In some instances, you are going to be able to select your linens, and there are a variety of styles and colors available. You may also be able to select the napkins, which is similar to the linens as well as the chairs. There are a variety of chairs or chair covers depending on the market to select from. Chair cover selections are normally colors similar to the linen colors, and the chair tie, the sash that goes at the top of the chair, can be selected for each wedding. Some of the most common chairs to choose from would be wood folding, chivari, ballroom, and ghost.

The classic linen or the least expensive to rent is going to be a poly cotton blend. These are most commonly seen in restaurants, and most rental companies have these in a variety of colors and shades. For example, in purple, there might be a lilac, then a purple, and an eggplant, so a light, a medium, and a dark.

The more common expensive linens are Lamour or Satin, which are the shiny linens. Shantung is also one of the shiny linens; however, the color of these makes them less shiny, and they have a more finished and polished look. Bengaline linens are slightly shiny and have some texture on them. Pintuck looks like a repetition of squares, and Crinkle, Crush, or Twist are not as shiny but have a rough, random texture pattern on them.

I always suggest having the linens floor length so that the legs of the tables are covered. It's a more finished and polished look.

Napkins, chair covers, and chair ties have the same configurations as the linens. Napkins and chair ties come in most of the styles linens do. Chair covers normally are in a classic or lamour material.

Chair selections are vast in most major wedding markets. The most common wedding chairs that you see in the movies are either a wood folding chair with a padded seat or a chivari chair with a cushion. Folding chairs are typically the least expensive and come in a variety of colors, including white, black, natural wood, fruitwood, or ivory. The cushion on the chair is attached and the same color as the chair itself. Chivari chairs are the ones that come in a variety of different colors: white, black, natural wood, silver, fruitwood, or clear. What is great about these chairs is that their seat cushion can be changed out to match the linen or the napkin you are using. It is a great customization piece; however, you must know that changing out the color might increase the price of the chair.

Other common chairs are ballroom or opera chairs. These have a more traditional look to them, and again, you have the ability to change out the chair cushion. Ghost chairs are clear and super modern. Some companies have them with a cushion that can be changed, and some of these chairs may have arms as well.

That is the base of your design—the table. Now, what goes on the table has to coordinate with your floral arrangements, dress colors, and personal flowers.

Now for the design of the personal flowers, ceremony elements, and reception pieces.

PERSONAL FLOWERS
(Items may not apply to all couples)

- **Bride** – Asking for pictures of bouquets is key. In order to get inside a bride's head and understand what she is thinking, you have to see what she is wearing and what she has in mind. You have to remind her that her bouquet is an accent piece to her dress, almost like a great pair of earrings, necklace, or shoes. It is an accessory and should accessorize her dress, not cover it up! These tend to be not colorful, rather white. However, I have done plenty of colorful bouquets for brides over the years! Again, it is all about what the bride wants!

- **Groom** – The groom's boutonniere should be something pulled from the bride's bouquet. Remember, nothing too big as the groom will be hugging everyone, and that flower will be smashed. Some florists give a second boutonniere for the groom if the ceremony will take place during the day in case the first gets ruined.

- **Bridesmaids** – These bouquets can and should be colorful to accentuate the colors of the wedding.

- **Groomsmen** – Like the groom, these boutonnieres should be a flower or two to match those being used in the bridesmaids' bouquets.

- **Ushers** – Typically, the ushers get something similar to the groomsmen, if not the same thing.

- **Ring Bearer** – Depending on his age, either a boutonniere is appropriate or, if he is too young, just the pillow is okay! REMEMBER, the rings should be with the best man, and the ring bearer should have faux rings to carry down the aisle, just in case!

- **Flower Girl** – They normally carry either a basket of rose petals that are thrown down the aisle (check with the ceremony location and make sure that this is allowed) or they can carry mini-bouquets or pomanders.

- **Mothers' Corsages** – Normally, these are flowers from the bride's bouquet or something that is white or ivory. I recommend going with a wrist corsage as pin corsages normally poke holes in their dresses. That is not a good way to start off the day! I would ask the mothers if they want a wrist or pin corsage or if they just want to carry a nosegay.
- **Fathers' Boutonnieres** – Again, these are normally white and something that matches the mother's corsage.
- **Grandmothers' Corsages** – This is normally similar to the mothers' corsages.
- **Grandfathers' Boutonnieres** – This is normally similar to the fathers' boutonnieres.
- **Godparents (Male & Female)** – These are similar to but smaller than the parents' and grandparents' corsages.
- **Readers** – This can be a boutonniere or a wrist corsage, again something small that might match the wedding party.

CEREMONY

- **Altar Arrangements (Christian or Church Weddings)** – This is something that you use primarily as two pieces to flank the altar in a church. These can be used in either a church or a venue/hotel to create a ceremonious atmosphere for the wedding. Normally, these can be repurposed at the wedding reception on the place card table, gift table, dessert station, or somewhere else to save on cost.
- **Chuppah (Jewish Weddings)** – A Chuppah is a canopy that a traditional Jewish Wedding takes place under. This is can be either a stable structure or could be movable and has four posts with the top covered. The florist usually will provide this.

- **Mandap (Hindu Weddings)** – A Mandap is a canopy that a traditional Hindu Wedding takes place under.

- **Pew Flowers** – In churches, flowers are often used to decorate the pews, depending on budget and the church rules. If you are having the wedding ceremony at the venue, you can look at repurposing the table arrangements to use on the aisle for décor. If you do this, it is important to have a ribbon or fabric that will block the guests from entering and exiting the rows of chairs on the main aisle. They will have to enter and exit on the outside aisle.

- **Aisle Runner** – There are a couple things to consider. Depending on where the ceremony is, there are different rules you will have to follow. Some churches do not allow aisle runners. Some churches will make you pre-set the runner, and if that is the case, you have to block off the center aisle and then have the guests enter on the side aisles. You can also have the runner pulled just before the bride comes down the aisle. (I do not advise this as I have seen too many mishaps with it!) If you are in a venue or hotel, most likely it will be pre-laid where it will be a heavier cloth and will have to have the aisle sectioned off so the guests do not walk on it. Keep in mind that the surface where it is placed is going to be on tile or carpet, so you need to consider how it will be fastened so it holds as many people as it has to for those who will walk down the aisle. Also, if you are making an aisle and there will be three people at any one time walking down the aisle or if the bride has a large dress, you will have to make it double wide. That is where they lay two aisle runners side by side, and in the center of those two, they lay a third on top of it, creating a double wide aisle.

- **Catholic Ceremonies, Parent Presentation Flowers & for The Virgin Mary** – In Catholic wedding ceremonies, there are two additional items that the florist will provide. One is the parent presentation flowers. These are normally single roses or small bouquets that are presented to the mother of the bride and the mother of the groom during the sign of peace. Then there is also a small bouquet that is presented to the Virgin Mary Statue after the communion ends, normally where the "Ave Maria" is played and the bride leaves this small bouquet of roses as an offering during that part of the ceremony.

RECEPTION

- **Place Card Table:** Place card tables or escort card tables are normally placed somewhere near the entrance of the cocktail reception or the ceremony space. With a card table, you have to make sure you understand if you have just one seating card. Tented cards are more traditionally created and called escort cards. That card will have the guest's name and a table number. When the guest arrives at the table, there will be an assigned seat for the guest. This is not always the case. When the actual seats at the table are not assigned, then you just have an escort card or a place card. Determine whether you would like to have the card table in a spot where the guests can retrieve their cards before the ceremony or whether they have to be out during the ceremony. Make sure the table is not in a place that will cause a traffic jam either. When it comes to floral, this table normally features a statement piece. Sometimes altar arrangements from the church can be repurposed. If not, this is a larger piece that will be considered a focal point for the guests to be welcomed by, so this will normally be a large piece.

- **Gift Card Table:** Usually this features just a gift card box or a bird cage with some flowers on it. I would not get crazy with décor here. This is a place to do minimal or none!

- **Guest Book Table:** I like to use a 30" round highboy table so the guests do not have to bend over to sign the book. Typically, candles and/or loose blooms will be enough on this table.

- **Highboy & Cabaret Tables:** These are your cocktail tables; normally what is done is either candles or a small arrangement on them. Make sure you check and see if the hotel or club provides candles. If they are provided, make sure the florist knows that so the client is not double charged.

- **Head Table or Sweet Heart Table:** There are a couple ways to design the floral arrangements for a head table or sweet heart table. If you have bouquets you can repurpose them as arrangements on this table and have the florist bring some cylinder vases to put in and some candles that will work. You can also have a lush arrangement of flowers on this table. Remember, to make sure whatever you do, for it to be low to the table so the guests can see the couple. If you have a head table or a harvest table, there will most likely be special arrangements designed for those tables. Again, just make sure where the couple will sit that they are not

- **Guest Tables:** There are so many different ways to design the flower arrangements for the reception. My method is to have the couple send me photos of arrangements that they like and ones that they do not like. I take those photos and learn the direction that they are headed in. From there I know who to go take them to see. I like to visit at least the florist, have a detailed meeting and make sure the couple feels comfortable with the decision. Ultimately, the client will make the choice on the flowers, but you can work with your florist to create. I typically, for budget purposes, like to put together two looks: one tall and one low. The elevated arrangements make a room look elegant and expensive, while the lows will be more cost effective and still interesting. Remember, you can also work with your florist to design and create these centerpieces to go down the aisle for the ceremony as long as the ceremony and the reception are in the same location!

- **Dessert Stations:** Repurpose altar arrangements or something from the ceremony. This way you may not need to do anything at all!

- **Bars:** Most of the time we do not worry about this, but if the client would like something, you can. Just be careful with candles! You do not want a bartender's sleeve to catch on fire.

Final touches that are added in for designing a room are lighting and draping elements. Let's start with lighting. There are a few different types of lighting that are used at events:

- *Uplighting* – Uplighting is where the lighting fixture is placed on the floor, right against the wall, and it washes up onto the wall and onto the ceiling. There are a quite a few different types of lighting fixtures that are used for uplighting; the two most common are par can and LED. Par cans are sort of the older fixture that is less common these days, but some companies still use them. The more common of the two are LED light fixtures. Both do the same thing, but the LED lighting has more color options and tend to have more modern conveniences.

- *Pinspotting* – Pinspotting is where small spot lights are either inserted into a room's existing lighting grid or are set up on lighting trees that are brought into the room and are to act as spot lights on the center of each guest table arrangement. Sometimes not all of the arrangements are spotted, just the taller ones. This is normally done in white light.

- *Room Wash* – Room washes are where lighting fixtures are mounted to either a lighting tree or affixed to the ceiling and are aimed all around the room and walls and typically washed with a color or pattern.

When it comes to draping elements or fabric backdrops, typically these are used for two reasons at a wedding. The first would be to be a backdrop for the ceremony. This typically creates a more elegant or soft background for the actual wedding ceremony. The other place that this is used would be behind a head table. Again, they create a soft backdrop, which is great for photos.

 *Notes*

Linen
- Cheapest is poly cotton blend
- Lamour or satin = $$
- Floor length linen = more finished look
- Napkins, chair covers, chair ties
should match the chairs
- wood w/ padded seat = cheapest
- Ballroom chairs (not cute)
    - More traditional
        * sweetseats.com ❀
- Ghost chairs
    - modern
    - clear
Ceremony Flowers
- Alter Arrangement
- Chuppah (Jewish)
- Mandap (Hindu)
- Pew Flowers
- Aisle runner
- Catholic Ceremonies

Notes

Chapter 7

Capturing the Moments in Real Time: Photography & Videography

Photography and videography

*T*hese are <u>two of the most important professionals</u> that the couple will hire when it comes to thinking about after the wedding is all over! You have to make sure you align yourself with some great photographers and videographers. They are the ones who will be able to capture the memories from the wedding. There are some items that you have to address with your client in order to get an idea of pricing:

- *Number of hours the photographer and videographer will be needed.* Typically, coverage is at <u>least eight hours</u>, but that depends on the schedule of events for the day. Later in this chapter, I will outline two short schedules that you can use to reference in planning the day of the wedding to know how to schedule the photographer.

All day = 10-12 hrs.

- *Number of Photographers*. Most times it is recommended to have two photographers. There are just so many advantages to having two photographers shooting the wedding. You have more coverage opportunities with two! But again, this might depend on budget and how the day goes. If the day is less spread out, then one shooter may be enough. If it is a longer day, then for sure two photographers!

- *Albums*. All photographers do different types of albums. You will have to discuss this with your photographers and your clients.

- *Schedule*. What you are going to see below is a simple break out of the timing of a photographer with key moments throughout the day. This is to give you an idea of how to schedule the photographer and how many hours you will need coverage.

Scheduling for the Day of the Wedding

There are two basic schedules that you will see on a wedding day. Below are two possible versions. One is where the ceremony will take place in the middle of the day and the couple does not see one another before the wedding, and the other is where the couple sees one another before the wedding and then the ceremony takes place later in the day.

- Day of Schedule (Schedule I)
  - Pre-Ceremony Preparation 1:30 p.m.
  - First Look 2:45 p.m.
  - Photos Around Town 3:15 p.m.
  - Family Photos 5 p.m.
  - Ceremony 6 p.m.
  - Reception 6:30 p.m. to 12:00 a.m. (coverage will end around 9:30 or 10:00 p.m.)
- Day of Schedule (Schedule II)
  - Pre-Ceremony Preparation 1:00 p.m.
  - Ceremony 3:00 p.m.

- Family Photos 4:00 p.m.
- Photos Around Town 4:30 to 5:45 p.m.
- Reception 6:00 p.m. to 12:00 a.m. (coverage will end around 9:30 or 10:00 p.m.)

Photo Instructions

When you work with a professional, you will really not have to worry about this. What you are going to see below is a list of what the photographer is most likely going to be capturing at each part of the process.

Pre-Ceremony Preparation (Items may not apply to all couples)

- Of dress
- Of shoes
- Of jewelry
- Of hair & make-up prep
- Accessories
- Of Suit or Tuxedo
- Getting into the dress
- Final prep in getting into suit or tuxedo.

First Look

- Have the couple, private or public, meet for the first time. Stay out of the way! This is not about you, and you do not need to be in the shot!

Location Shots (Around Town)

- Predetermined locations with photographer with bride, groom, and wedding party. Mostly group shots with the wedding party.

Family Photographs (Items may not apply to all couples)

- Couple
- Wedding Party

- Bride's Family with the Couple
- Groom's Family with the Couple
- Parents with the Couple
- Grandparents with the Couple

Ceremony

- Processional
- Readings
- Vows
- Rings
- Recessional

The Wedding Reception

- Cocktail Hour
  - Guests mingling
  - Hors d'oeuvres
  - Specialty cocktails
  - Place card table
  - Cake table
- Dinner and Dancing Reception (Items may not apply to all couples)
  - Wedding party announcements
  - Toasts
  - Dinner entrees (plated)
  - Thank you speech by the Couple
  - Cake cutting
  - First dance
  - Father/Daughter dance
  - Mother/Son dance
  - All dancing by the guests
  - Dessert/Cake table

Notes

All day package

(8 hrs?)

9:30 - last
9:45 - Sparklers
(10:00 Exit) → 11:00 p

Notes

Chapter 8

Let Them Eat Cake, or Cupcakes, or Delicious Desserts!

This is one of the sweetest and most fun parts of planning the wedding—the CAKE or the CUPCAKES! What we talk about in this section is more basic in outline form. Work with professionals to work with your client as there are so many different flavors and designs that can be created.

Cake

- The Look: something more contemporary or modern or something more traditional or romantic
- Color Scheme
    - This should be related to your overall color scheme for the wedding.
- Determine
    - Number of Tiers Needed?

- Pattern on the Cake?
- Ribbon around the layers and color?
- Cake Topper
  - This is something that the couple will purchase if they choose, or you can have the florist or décor company provide fresh blooms for the cake.
- Cake Plateau or Cake Stand
  - This is something that is normally not provided by the bakery but can be rented through your caterer.
- Cake Flavors
- Cake Filling
- Cake Frosting

Cupcakes

- The Look: something more contemporary or modern or something more traditional or romantic
- Color Scheme (May not be applicable depending on bakery)
- Regular Size or Minis
  - What is great about minis is that you can do a larger assortment of flavors.
- Cupcake Flavors
  - Every bakery or cupcakerie has their own selection of what they have to offer. Take a look at their menus online and see what they have to offer and if that is what your client is looking for.
- Cupcake Display

Dessert Station

- Creating a dessert display is fun. This can be a variety of options from a local bakery or it can come from the caterer or the venue. See what the couple would like and determine your options from there!

Notes

Notes

Chapter 9

Enhancing Natural Beauty with Hair Stylists & Make-Up Artists

(Items may not apply to all couples)

What you have to consider in booking hair and make-up services with your bride is how many people there will be for hair and make-up, where the location of the services will be, the timing and scheduling (most reliable hair and make-up studios will do this; you just need to let them know what time you will need to have the bride and wedding party ready!), and what are the day of wedding requirements of the artists and stylists. Take a look below as a check list for your planning these services out.

- Number of People for Hair
  - Bride
  - Bridesmaids
  - Mothers
  - Family Members
- Number of People for Make-Up
  - Bride

- Bridesmaids
- Mothers
- Family Members
- Timing and Schedule
  - Determine the arrival times of the hair stylist(s) & make-up artist(s) with their approval.
  - Again, working with the hair and make-up professionals, together you determine and agree on the start of services for the bride, wedding party, and any other family members have their hair and make-up applied as well as the all-important completion time.
  - If the ceremony is later in the day, have the mothers and other family members have the services after the bride and the bridesmaids. If the ceremony is in the afternoon, you may have to add an additional stylist to get everyone ready on time.
  - Allow 35–45 minutes per service per person. Allow two hours for the bride to get her hair and make-up done.

Day of Requirements

Most likely, the hair and make-up artists will have a list of what they will need for the day of the wedding. Here are just a few of the items they may require.

- Number of Chairs
- Type of Chairs – Barstools
- Power Requirements
- Extension Cords
- Lighting

Planner Tips

- Have the ladies wear a button down shirt or something that goes over the head easily.
- Have the bride brush her teeth before her lipstick gets put on or make-up begins.

Notes

Notes

Chapter 10

Booking the Overnight Accommodations at a Hotel

This section takes a short review of what you need to ask in order to help put together a hotel room block.

- Type of hotel, contemporary, modern, traditional
- Price range: low, medium, high
- Number of rooms for the Couple (day before included)
- Number of rooms for family
- Number of rooms for wedding party
- Number of expected out of town guests
- Hospitality suite. This is a room that some hotels will offer that can be used by the family to offer food and beverages for their out of town guests and a place to gather, and it can be used for preparation.

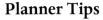
Planner Tips

- Book a hotel without an attrition clause. This is where your client will not be financially responsible for any sleeping rooms that are not booked.

- Most hotels will start with 10 rooms in the block and will add as needed.

- They will set up a phone number to call or a website for the guests to make reservations.

- Book hotels accordingly. Watch convention schedules to see what additional shows may be in town that might affect room rates.

- Guests may be able to book hotel rooms on other websites at a better price than the block.

Notes

Notes

Chapter 11

Musicians for the Wedding Ceremony

(Items may not apply to all couples)

The ceremony music is different from reception music. Again, working with a band or trio or quartet, they will work through these items with your client. However, for your reference, this is what they will be asking your client. Your band or DJ may provide the music, or you may have to outsource a soloist, duo, trio, or quartet. If the ceremony is at a church, check the policy at the church. Some require you to use their own musicians.

Ceremony Songs Normally Required

- Processional, Family & Wedding Party
- Processional, Bride
- Recessional, Bride, Groom, and all parties

Musician Set-Up Checklist

- Arrive 60 minutes prior to start time.

- 30 minutes before ceremony, begin playing prelude music.
- How many musicians?
- How many chairs will be needed?
- Will they need electric?
- Will there be a vocalist?

Notes

Notes

Chapter 12

Stationary & Invitations: The First Look of the Wedding the Guests Will See

So often I think that the invitations are overlooked. The way that I look at it is that this is the first thing the guests will see and will foreshadow what is to come at the wedding. Invitations should be an important part of the planning process. Now, you do not have to break the budget with the invitations; however, you should consider them to be an important aspect of the wedding.

The first thing is to determine the look: something more contemporary or modern or something more traditional or romantic. This should be in the same theme as your décor scheme.

- Contemporary or Modern
- Traditional
- Romantic

- Rustic

- Vintage

Decide color scheme. These colors should be in the same scheme as your décor scheme. Remember, they do not have to be perfectly matched; however, they need to be close!

- Color #1:

- Color #2:

- Color #3:

Stationary Items that have to be designed and mailed (See Chapter 2 for additional reference of each item)

- *Invitations* – This is the actual invitation to the wedding ceremony. If the wedding ceremony takes place at the same location as the reception, at the bottom of the invitation, it will say "Reception To Follow" and there will be no need for a Reception Card. Invitations should be mailed 2 to 2 and a half months before the wedding, response cards should be back 1 month before the wedding!

- *Reception Cards* – If the reception and ceremony are at two different locations, it is common to have an additional card known as the Reception Card that will have the name of the venue, address, and start time of the reception on it.

- *Response Cards* – These are the cards that are used by the guests that will be used to determine if they are coming to the wedding or not. If you need to have the couple give the caterer or venue a choice of entrée prior to the wedding day (which is highly common), there will be a place on this card that will give the guests the option to select their entrée.

- *Insert Card* – These are cards to give the guests the information on the hotel room block, transportation, possibly rehearsal dinner or day after wedding brunch.

- *Save the Dates* – These are used to send out to guests anywhere from 1 year to 6 months before the wedding to let them know the date of the wedding.
- *Thank You Notes* – After the wedding, the couple will have to say, "Thank you"!
- *Stamps*
- *Calligraphy*

For the Ceremony:

- Programs

For the Reception:

- Table Numbers
- Escort Cards
- Place Cards
- Menu Cards
- Calligraphy

Number of Guests Invited:

Divide guest count by half and add about 30 extra invitations and save the dates to determine ordering quantities.

Notes

Notes

Chapter 13

Getting Married...Isn't That What It Is All About?

One of the most important parts of a wedding is THE WEDDING! This is the part that makes it official, where the couple goes from engaged to really married! Now, working with a couple in a church, most times, the church is going to tell you how they would like the ceremony to go. When you go into their house, you have to follow their rules. When you have the opportunity to do a wedding "on-site" at the reception venue, or in a park, in front of a fountain, or somewhere else outside of a church, you and your client get to design the wedding ceremony.

If you have a wedding outside of a church, you are going to have to hire an ordained officiant or minister or judge to perform the ceremony. In that case, the typical ceremony outline looks like this:

- Outline of the Ceremony
  - The Processional of the Grandparents, Wedding Party and Couple
  - Gathering Words

- Opening Prayers
- Words to the Couple
- Support from Families and Friends
- Readings
- Vows
- Exchange of Rings
- Pronouncement of Couple
- Benediction or Closing Words
- Presentation of Couple
- Ceremony Processional & Recessional Scenarios

This is what the marriage officiant is there to do. Let him or her help your couple work through the ceremony and the items that they want to include. This is the most sacred part of the wedding. Include yourself as much as your client asks you to.

Examples of Ceremony Processionals & Recessionals

Where you can be helpful is in assisting the couple with designing and creating the processional (entrance into the ceremony) and the recessional (exit from the ceremony). On the next few pages, you will see examples you can use in your design process.

Please note, in the following scenarios, these will not pertain to all couples.

Scenario #1

Ceremony to begin

Processional

- Officiant & the Groom to begin at the front

Music to begin

- Grandparents of the Bride
- Grandparents of the Groom

    (GRANDPARENTS CAN GO BEFORE THE ACTUAL PROCESSIONAL)

- Mother of the Bride, Escorted by ESCORT NAME
- Parents of the Groom
- Groomsman #5 & Bridesmaid #5
- Groomsman #4 & Bridesmaid #4
- Groomsman #3 & Bridesmaid #3
- Groomsman #2 & Bridesmaid #2
- Groomsman #1 & Bridesmaid #1
- Maid or Matron of Honor & Best Man

Music Changes

- Bride and her father walk in

Ceremony Begins

Ceremony to Conclude

Recessional

Music to begin

- Bride & Groom
- Maid or Matron of Honor & Best Man
- Groomsman #1 & Bridesmaid #1
- Groomsman #2 & Bridesmaid #2
- Groomsman #3 & Bridesmaid #3

- Groomsman #4 & Bridesmaid #4
- Groomsman #5 & Bridesmaid #5
- Parents of the Groom
- Parents of the Bride
- Grandparents to follow

Notes

Scenario #2

Processional

- Officiant to make way to the front with groom and groomsmen down a side aisle before the music begins.

ORDER DEPENDS ON HOW THEY ARE ENTERING. DEPENDING ON ENTRANCE, SOMETIMES GROOMSMAN #5 WOULD BE THE FIRST ONE TO GO AND THE REVEREND WOULD BE THE LAST TO GO.

- Groom
- Best Man
- Groomsman # 1
- Groomsman # 2
- Groomsman #3
- Groomsman #4
- Groomsman #5

Music begins once all groomsmen are in place.

- Grandparents of the Bride
- Grandparents of the Groom

  (GRANDPARENTS CAN GO BEFORE THE ACTUAL PROCESSIONAL)

- Mother of the Bride, Escorted by ESCORT NAME
- Bridesmaid #5
- Bridesmaid #4
- Bridesmaid #3
- Bridesmaid #2
- Bridesmaid #1
- Maid or Matron of Honor

Music Changes

- Bride and her father to walk in

Ceremony Begins

Ceremony to Conclude

Recessional

Music to begin

- BRIDE'S NAME & GROOM'S NAME
- Maid or Matron of Honor & Best Man
- Groomsman #1 & Bridesmaid #1
- Groomsman #2 & Bridesmaid #2
- Groomsman #3 & Bridesmaid #3
- Groomsman #4 & Bridesmaid #4
- Groomsman #5 & Bridesmaid #5
- Parents of the Groom
- Parents of the Bride
- Grandparents to follow

Notes

Scenario #3

Ceremony to begin

Processional

Music to begin

- Grandparents of the Bride
- Grandparents of the Groom

  (GRANDPARENTS CAN GO BEFORE THE ACTUAL PROCESSIONAL)
- Mother of the Bride, Escorted by ESCORT NAME
- Parents of the Groom
- Officiant and the Groom and Groomsmen Enter
- Bridesmaid #5
- Bridesmaid #4
- Bridesmaid #3
- Bridesmaid #2
- Bridesmaid #1
- Maid or Matron of Honor

Music Changes

- Bride and her father to walk in

Ceremony Begins

Ceremony to Conclude

Recessional

Music to begin

Bride & Groom

Maid or Matron of Honor & Best Man

- Groomsman #1 & Bridesmaid #1
- Groomsman #2 & Bridesmaid #2
- Groomsman #3 & Bridesmaid #3

- Groomsman #4 & Bridesmaid #4
- Groomsman #5 & Bridesmaid #5
- Parents of the Groom
- Parents of the Bride
- Grandparents to follow

Notes

Scenario #4

Ceremony to begin

Processional

Music to begin

- Grandparents of the Bride
- Grandparents of the Groom

  (GRANDPARENTS CAN GO BEFORE THE ACTUAL PROCESSIONAL)

- Mother of the Bride, Escorted by ESCORT NAME
- Parents of the Groom
- Officiant and the Groom and Groomsmen Enter
- **Mothers Light Unity Candle**
- Bridesmaid #5
- Bridesmaid #4
- Bridesmaid #3
- Bridesmaid #2
- Bridesmaid #
- Maid or Matron of Honor

Music Changes

- Bride and her father to walk in

Ceremony Begins

Ceremony to Conclude

Recessional

Music to begin

- Bride & Groom
- Maid or Matron of Honor & Best Man
- Groomsman #1 & Bridesmaid #1
- Groomsman #2 & Bridesmaid #2

- Groomsman #3 & Bridesmaid #3
- Groomsman #4 & Bridesmaid #4
- Groomsman #5 & Bridesmaid #5
- Parents of the Groom
- Parents of the Bride

Notes

Scenario #5

Ceremony to begin

Processional

Music to begin

- Officiant to enter
- Couple #5
- Couple #4
- Couple #3
- Couple #2
- Couple #1
- Best Men or Maids or Matrons of Honor
- Flower Girls and Ring Bearers

Music Changes

- Groom #1 and his parents to walk in
- Groom #2 and his parents to walk in

  OR

- Bride #1 and his parents to walk in
- Bride #2 and his parents to walk in

Ceremony Begins

Ceremony to Conclude

Recessional

Music to begin

- The Couple
- Maids or Matrons of Honor or Best Men
- Couple #1
- Couple #2
- Couple #3
- Couple #4

- Couple #5
- Parents of the Groom #1
- Parents of the Groom #2

  Or

- Parents of the Bride #1
- Parents of the Bride #2

Notes

Chapter 14

The Night before the Wedding: The Rehearsal Dinner

The rehearsal dinner is something that is typically hosted by the evening before the wedding. Nowadays, it can happen two evenings before the wedding as well. This is typically a less formal gathering but still something nice for the couple, their immediate families, and the wedding party. In some instances, when there are quite a few out of town guests, they might be invited as well. Or a separate cocktail reception may be organized at the host hotel for a large number of out of town guests.

Here is a guide to use in planning a couple's rehearsal dinner.

Food and beverage is onsite at the venue; you select and work with the catering rep to help create a menu that you work with that makes your clients happy!

Dinner Questions

- Number of Guests (Count Adults and Children)
- Location – What Venue?

- Start Time / End Time
- Cocktail Hour (Duration)
  - Passed Hors D'oeuvres
  - Passed Wine & Water
  - Open Bar
  - Specialty Drinks
  - Food Stations
- Dinner Service
  - Plated Dinner (Number of Courses – Soup / Appetizer, Salad, Entrée, Dessert)
  - Family Style
  - Buffet
  - Food Stations / Cocktail Style
  - Wine Service with Dinner?
  - Champagne Toast with Dinner?
  - Dessert & Coffee Served Tableside or Stations

Check with the restaurant or venue. Most of the time they have a standard package of menus that can be used for a rehearsal dinner that includes two to three courses and a liquor package. Remember, most people are not going to drink too much at the rehearsal dinner, so more focus should be placed on the food and less on the alcohol!

Chapter 15

BYOB for the Wedding Day

*T*here are some venues out there that let couples bring their own liquor for their wedding day. This is great as it will save them some money and they get to customize their bar. In some markets, there is a local liquor distributor that you can work with, and some might even deliver, which is great! The way that I approach selecting liquor is first I ask the couple to send me a list of all of the liquor, beers, wines, and champagnes that they would like for the wedding. Typically, this is a good list to send them to prompt them to request specific brands.

Standard List:

- Vodka
- Gin
- Rum
- Tequila
- Bourbon
- Whiskey

- Scotch
- Cordials & Liquors
- Beer
- Wine: Red & White – Bar & Dinner Wines Different?
- Champagne

Then I send that information along with the answers to these questions to the liquor distributor.

- What are the total number of hours of the reception?
- How many guests will be attending the wedding?
- How many bars will there be throughout the evening?
- At any point, will there be any passed wine or champagne?
- Will there be a specialty drink?
- Will there be separate dinner wines than what is at the bar?
- Will there be a champagne toast?

With that information, an informed and experience liquor distributor or store should be able to give you the right quantities. I also then double check the order with the caterer to make sure the quantities of everything look correct.

Chapter 16

Smile for the Photo Booth!

The photo booth has taken the wedding industry by storm. It is more common than not to have a photo booth at a wedding these days. These are either actual booths, backdrops with a photographer, or a pipe and drape square that is used for the guests to step in and get their photos taken. There are normally props provided by the photo booth company as well as a signing book where the guests can order a copy of their photo(s) and then one for the couple. The couple's copies typically get glued into a scrap book where the guests can sign around their photo(s). These are often silly photos and best taken once everyone has had a cocktail or three! Hence, I always suggest the start time to be after dinner until the end of the wedding.

Some key suggestions with a photo booth:

- Having the booth close or in the same room as the dance floor is a good idea. This way the guests will go into the booth but will

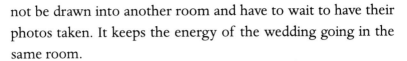
not be drawn into another room and have to wait to have their photos taken. It keeps the energy of the wedding going in the same room.

- You need to find out from the photo booth company what is included with their packages.
- Props?
- Signing book? This can be used in lieu of a guest book.
- Will they need tables? How many? What size? Will they need linens for the tables?

Chapter 17

Going Point to Point - Transportation!

One of the most challenging parts of a wedding can be the transportation. If you have to transport guests from a hotel to a church, to a reception, and then back to the hotel where they are staying, and there are 300 of them, it may cause some stress on your end. Never fear; it can be done, but it might take some time to get used to how to do this. The first step is having a reputable company or companies on hand to work with that actually do weddings every weekend. The transport companies I work with are fantastic because they shuttle weddings all the time.

There are different vehicles that you should be aware of that can be used on the day of the wedding.

- Sedan – This is normally for two people.

- Stretch Limo or Sedan – These tend to come in a few sizes and

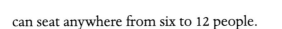

can seat anywhere from six to 12 people.

- Mini Buses – These are small coach buses that range in size and can seat somewhere between 12 to 40 people.
- Coach Buses – These are large motor coaches that seat somewhere between 50 to 60 guests.

Depending on the schedule of the day's events and happenings, the transportation is going to be different. Let's look at a few different scenarios on how the wedding day will time out.

Please note, in the following scenarios, these will not pertain to all couples.

Schedule 1:
Ceremony and Reception at the Same Location

The couple and wedding party will be preparing at a hotel or a home for the wedding day.

The first look between the couple will take place at the preparation location. Once that happens, the couple and the wedding party will depart for afternoon photographs.

Pick Up Vehicle for the Couple and Wedding Party

Photos Around Town (by Wedding Party Transport). Once this is complete, this vehicle will go to the wedding and reception venue with the wedding party and will drop them off. This vehicle may then be used to go pick up guests at the host hotel, or service may conclude.

Pick Up Vehicle for Family for Family Photos

Family photos will typically take place before the ceremony. If this is the case and you need to transport the couple's families, you will have to arrange for a vehicle to pick up all of the family members who have to be at the wedding and reception site early for these photos. The arrival time of the family should be the same as the wedding party's arrival time at the venue.

Pick Up Vehicle for Guests

There will be one or more vehicles that will be needed to pick up all of the guests at the host hotel and bring them to the wedding and reception site. Make sure you have enough seats for each guest! These vehicles should pick up the guests about an hour before the wedding, giving you anywhere from one hour to 45 minutes before the ceremony start time to get them to the venue.

Evening Shuttle

One of the most common ways to transport guests at the end of the evening is to set up shuttle service between one or more vehicles to bring guests from the venue to the host hotel. I suggest having one or more vehicles, not to have scheduled times but to have them shuttle as needed with one shuttle to be 30 minutes before the end of the wedding, making sure all of the vehicles are back at the end time and leave 15 minutes after the official end time of the wedding.

Notes

Schedule 2:
Ceremony and Reception at Different Locations

Please note, in the following scenarios, these will not pertain to all couples.

The couple and wedding party will be preparing at a hotel or a home for the wedding day. From here, the bride and the bridesmaids and the groom and the groomsmen will go to the ceremony site separately. Sometimes, the bride's family will go with the bride and the groom's parents will go with him. The pickup for everyone will be at the host hotel or preparation location.

Pick Up for Bride & Bridesmaids & Bride's Family

This vehicle is typically large enough for the entire wedding party and will be used after the ceremony.

Pick Up for Groom & Groomsmen & Groom's Family

This vehicle will just be used to bring everyone to the ceremony site, or it might take the immediate family (parents and grandparents) back to the host hotel in between the ceremony and reception.

Pick Up for Guests

There will be one or more vehicles needed to pick up all of the guests at the host hotel and bring them to the wedding and reception site. Make sure you have enough seats for each guest! These vehicles should pick up the guests about an hour before the wedding, giving you anywhere from one hour to 45 minutes before the ceremony start time to get them to the venue. Make sure that these vehicles wait during the ceremony and take the guests back to the host hotel after the wedding and then bring them over to the wedding reception later on that evening.

Following the ceremony, family photos will take place. The guests can get back in the vehicles that brought them to the ceremony site, one can wait for the family members, or the groom's vehicle can wait and bring the family back to the host hotel.

The wedding party will board and take the bride and the bridesmaids' transport vehicle that brought them to the ceremony. From here, they will take wedding party photos. When they are finished, the wedding party vehicle drops them off at the reception.

Guests board the vehicles that took them to the ceremony and that will proceed to drop them off at the reception site.

Evening Shuttle

One of the ways that is most common at the end of the evening is to set up shuttle service between one or more vehicles to bring guests from the venue to the host hotel. I suggest having one or more vehicles, not to have scheduled times but to have them shuttle as needed with a shuttle 30 minutes before the end of the wedding, making sure all of the vehicles are back at the end time and leave 15 minutes after the official end time of the wedding.

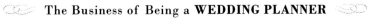

Notes

How Is the Day Going to Time Out? Creating a Wedding Day Timeline and Other Details for the Day

One of the most important pieces of the wedding planning process is to create a detailed wedding day timeline. There are a few key elements that have to be discussed and integrated into your wedding day timeline and notes. This first set is looking at a wedding day timeline with the ceremony and reception at the same location.

Please note, in the following scenarios, these will not pertain to all couples.

- Breakfast Service
- Arrival of Hair and Make-up Teams
- Schedule of wedding party members having their hair and make-up

done. Each service may take up to 45 minutes per person, per service.

- Lunch Service
- Arrival Time of Photographer
- Arrival Time of Personal Flowers
- Dress Time of the Bridesmaids
- Dress Time of the Groom and Groomsmen
- Dress Time of the Bride
- First Look Time
- Transportation Arrival Time for Wedding Party
- Photo Locations
- Vendor Load-in Times (Catering, DJ, Band, Décor, Bakery, Photo Booth)
- Transportation Pick Up Time for Family
- Wedding Party Arrival Time at Venue
- Family Arrival Time at Venue
- Family Photo Time
- Guest Transportation Pick Up Time
- Order of Ceremony Processional
- Ceremony Start Time
- Ceremony End Time
- Cocktail Hour Timing
- Reception Timing, including wedding party introductions, toasts and speeches, blessing, first dance, dances with parents, cake cutting, and thank you by bride and groom, plus any other happenings
- Evening Shuttle Start Time
- Late Night Snack Service
- Last Call
- Wedding End Time

Here is a tentative timeline with a first look and ceremony and reception at the same location.

MID TO LARGE SIZE WEDDING PARTY

- 9:00 a.m. Hair and make-up service begin. (Breakfast is brought into the room.)
- 12:00 p.m. Lunch to be served. (Brought in normally, delivery or room service)
- 1:00 p.m. Photographer to arrive
- 2:00 p.m. Hair and make-up completed
- 2:30 p.m. Bride to be dressed
- 2:30 p.m. Groom to be dressed
- 2:45 p.m. Staged meeting of the Couple
- 3:00 p.m. Get on bus for photos around town
- 4:30–5:15 p.m. Couple and The Wedding Party arrive at venue; family arrives and family formal photos are taken
- 5:30 p.m. Guests begin to arrive
- 6:00 p.m. Ceremony to begin
- 6:30 p.m. Ceremony to conclude
- 6:30–7:30 p.m. Cocktail hour
- 7:30–8:00p.m. Wedding party announcements, toasts (limit of three), dinner service to begin
- 9:00 p.m. Cake cutting, first dance, father/daughter, mother/son; dessert station opens
- 10:30 p.m. Late night snack
- 11:45 p.m. Last call!
- 12:00 p.m. Wedding to conclude

For a wedding with a small wedding party or none, start around 10:00 a.m. or 11:00 a.m.

This next list is for when the couple is having a ceremony and reception at different locations.

Please note, in the following scenarios, these will not pertain to all couples.

- Arrival of Hair and Make-up Teams
- Schedule of wedding party members having their hair and make-up done. Each service may take up to 45 minutes per person, per service.
- Lunch Service
- Arrival Time of Photographer
- Arrival Time of Personal Flowers
- Dress Time of the Bridesmaids
- Dress Time of the Groom and Groomsmen
- Dress Time of the Bride
- Arrival Time of Bride's Transportation at the host hotel and the ceremony location
- Arrival Time of the Groom's Transportation at the host hotel and the ceremony location
- Transportation Arrival Time for the guests at the host hotel and the ceremony location
- Order of Ceremony Processional
- Ceremony Start Time
- Family Photos post ceremony
- Departure time and destination for guest transportation
- Departure time and destination for family transportation
- Departure time and destinations for the Wedding Party
- Vendor Load-in Times (Catering, DJ, Band, Décor, Bakery, Photo Booth)
- Transportation Pick Up Time for Family and Guests to bring

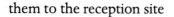

them to the reception site

- Wedding Party Arrival Time at Venue
- Reception Start Time
- Cocktail Hour Timing
- Reception Timing, including wedding party introductions, toasts and speeches, blessing, first dance, dances with parents, cake cutting, and thank you by bride and groom, plus any other happenings
- Evening Shuttle Start Time
- Late Night Snack Service
- Last Call
- Wedding End Time

Here is a tentative timeline with the ceremony at a church or afternoon ceremony and a reception in the evening.

MID TO LARGE SIZE WEDDING PARTY

- 9:00 a.m. Hair and make-up service begin. (Breakfast is brought into the room.)
- 12:00 p.m. Lunch to be served. (Brought in normally, delivery or room service)
- 1:00 p.m. Photographer to arrive
- 1:30 p.m. Hair and make-up conclude
- 1:45 p.m. Groom to be dressed
- 2:00 p.m. Bride to be dressed
- 2:00–2:15 p.m. Bride & Bridesmaids depart from hotel to church groom
- 2:30 p.m. Guests begin to arrive
- 3:00 p.m. Ceremony to begin
- 4:00 p.m. Ceremony to conclude – Family Photos after church

ceremony

- 4:15 p.m. Get on bus for photos around town
- 5:15–5:45 p.m. Bride and party arrive at venue
- 6:00–7:00 p.m. Cocktail hour
- 7:00–7:30 p.m. Wedding Party announcements, toasts (limit of three), dinner service to begin
- 9:00 p.m. Cake cutting, first dance, father/daughter, mother/son; dessert station opens
- 10:30 p.m. Late night snack
- 11:45 p.m. Last call!
- 12:00 p.m. Wedding to conclude

For a wedding with a small wedding party or none, start around 10:00 a.m. or 11:00 a.m.

It is good to have more information from your couple and to integrate it into the wedding day timeline and your notes.

Family Information

Collecting the names of the family and wedding party is key. Make sure you have the first and last names of the people who are a part of your couple's big day.

- Bride's Family
  - Parents
  - Stepparents
  - Siblings
  - Grandparents
- Groom's Family
  - Parents
  - Stepparents
  - Siblings
  - Grandparents

- Wedding Party
  - Maid/Matron of Honor
  - Bridesmaids
  - Jr. Bridesmaids
  - Best Man
  - Groomsmen
  - Ring Bearer
  - Flower Girl
  - Ushers
  - Readers

PERSONAL ITEM CHECKLIST

These are the items that you will most likely be responsible for tracking during the day of the wedding.

Ceremony Items

- Programs
- Rings
- Marriage License
- Unity Candle or Sand Ceremony Items
- Religious Items

Reception Items

- Place Cards (in alpha order)
- Guest Book
- Pen
- Gift Card Box
- Menu Cards
- Table Numbers
- Toasting Flutes
- Cake Knife & Server
- Favors

- Washroom Baskets
- Beverage Napkins
- Restroom Hand Towels

VENDOR CONTACT INFORMATION

Making sure you have the names, cell phone numbers, and e-mail addresses of all of the vendors for the wedding day.

- Caterer
- Bakery
- Florist and/or Event Design
- Hair Stylist
- Invitations and Stationary
- Liquor Supplier
- Make-up Artist
- Music – Band or DJ
- Music – Instrumental
- Officiant
- Photo Booth
- Photographer
- Rehearsal Dinner
- Rentals
- Transportation
- Valet
- Venue
- Videographer

Notes

Notes

Chapter 19

The Final Checklist of Items for Your Clients to Secure with You!

*H*ere is a list of all of the final, final, final details that normally are asked and finalized about a month before the wedding.

Ceremony Music

Make all song selections for processional and recessional. There are typically two songs for the processional and one for the recessional.

- Processional Song 1, for family and wedding party
- Processional Song 2, for the bride's entrance
- Recession Song, for everyone's exit

Reception Music

These are the songs your couples will need to pick. I suggest they work with the DJ or the band to do this.

- Wedding Party Introductions

- Cake Cutting (or let band/DJ decide)
- First Dance
- Father/Daughter Dance
- Mother/Son Dance

Photography

- Preparation Shots. Typically, the photographer will take photos of the end of hair and make-up if at the hotel, as well as the dress, accessories, shoes, and the rings. If there is a second photographer, that photographer will be getting photos of the groom getting ready.
- Either First Look or off to the Church. The photographer and planner will help work a location at the hotel for a first look shot.
- Family Photos, either before or after depending on first look. It is best to type out a detailed list of people by first name who you would like to have photos taken of. That will be easier for the photographer to call names and have them waiting. Those family members should know when and where those photos are going to happen before the day of the wedding. A good time to tell them is at the rehearsal!

Gratuity

Determine which vendors get tipped, and decide on amounts and payment method.

- Catering Staff, Servers & Bartenders
- Catering Captain
- Kitchen Cooks
- Kitchen Chef
- Additional Vendors to Consider
- Hair Stylist

- Make-up Artist
- DJ or Band Members
- Photographer
- Videographer
- Catering Sales Representative
- Floral Representative
- Photo Booth
- Transport Drivers

With these vendors, we see a range from $50 to $200 per vendor.

PLEASE NOTE: Tipping is not expected. It is something that is done if you feel that your vendor went above and beyond their call of duty. If you tip, it will be graciously accepted.

Marriage License

Obtain license. All counties are different. Just make sure you receive the license in the county where the marriage ceremony is performed.

Guest Count

Final guest count will have to be given to both the venue/caterer and the florist.

Floor Plan/Seating Chart

Finalize with caterer and florist. This will determine the floor plan, how many tables you will have, and how many centerpieces you will have. This should be completed one month prior to the wedding to determine final payments to the caterer and florist.

Final Payments

Determine who will have to be paid. Most vendors are one month prior to seven days before.

Day of the Wedding Payments

Determine which, if any, vendors must be paid on the day of the wedding. Write checks or procure cash; put it in individually labeled envelopes for delivery by planner.

Place Cards

Create place cards, put in alphabetical order by last name (these can be made one per couple; does not have to be one per guest), label, and print out any special instructions.

Personal Items

Make sure client gathers personal items (flutes, cake knife and server, etc.), and keep them in original packaging or make sure they are well-packed and labeled.

Timeline

Finalize timeline two weeks before. Leave for the client by the week of the wedding.

Notes

Notes

Preparing for the Wedding Day and a Personal Guide on What You Need to Make It a Success!

*T*he wedding day is finally here. Are you ready? Here is a guide to what you need to think through to make the wedding day a success!

Let's start with you. What do you need to do to prepare for the wedding day?

- First thing, make sure you get enough rest the night before the wedding. The morning of, I do not have anything stressful planned. I am just relaxing and letting my mind rest before I have to get going.

- Have breakfast. You are not going to have too much time to eat during the day. Make sure you have some snacks. I love snack/

protein bars and bring those with me on the day of any wedding.

- Make sure you have your wedding day emergency kit packed. This consists of a few key items. The items I use the most are below:

  - Scissors
  - Sewing Kit
  - Double Sided Tape
  - Various Sized Safety Pins
  - Tissues

Here is a more complete list of items that are included in my personal wedding day kit:

- Lip Balm
- Lint Roller
- Shout Wipes
- Tide-to-Go Stick
- Gum/Mints
- Hand Lotion
- Deodorant
- Mini Disposable Toothbrushes
- Mouthwash
- Travel Manicure Set
- Q-Tips
- Hair Ties
- Bobby Pins
- Safety Pins
- Toothpicks
- Contact Solution
- Eye Drops
- Tampons
- Band-Aids
- Body Spray

- Hair Spray
- Hair Brush
- Comb
- Antacids

- Make sure you have comfortable shoes.

- Have an assistant for the day. Check in with each other in the morning and go over any changes or final details that came up at the wedding rehearsal the night before.

- You need to confirm with all of your vendors before the wedding. It is a nice touch when you know the room number of the hotel room where the preparations will be taking place and shoot an e-mail over to the hair and make-up team, the florist for personal flower delivery, and the photographer and videographer. Those are the only vendors that need to know!

- Give yourself plenty of time for getting yourself ready the morning of the wedding and to get to the preparation venue.

- Have your out of office message on your e-mail so you do not feel pressured to answer any emails from other clients or potential clients and they understand you are working at a wedding that day.

Throughout the day, here are some tips to help with the wedding day timeline. See my integrated notes that I use for my planner's timeline for the day of the wedding. This is my personal checklist that I use to help get us through the day. Let's start with a ceremony and reception at the same location.

- Have a schedule of wedding party members having their hair and make-up done. Each service may take up to 45 minutes per person, per service. Check in with the team and make sure everything is running on time. Kindly remind them of the time you need everyone dressed and out the door.

- Arrival Time of Photographer. Work with the photographer to get any of the detail items ready with them. This includes jewelry, shoes, purse, dress, suits, tuxedos, cufflinks, ties and any other items the bride and/or groom would like photographed. Do not get in the way; be there to help them have all of the items they need for these photos.

- Arrival Time of Personal Flowers. Thank them for being on time, and ask if you can assist in the pinning of the boutonnieres and distribution of any of the flowers.

- Dress Time of the Bridesmaids. Remind the ladies 30 minutes before they need to be dressed that they need to be dressed in 30 minutes.

- Dress Time of the Groom and Groomsmen. Remind the guys 30 minutes before they need to be dressed that they need to be dressed in 30 minutes.

- Dress Time of the Bride. Remind the bride before she gets dressed to brush her teeth and that this is her chance to use the restroom before she puts that gown on. It sounds silly, but it is a good idea!

- First Look Time. Work with the photographer to bring either the bride or the groom into place. Again, work as a team to do this.

- Transportation Arrival Time for the Wedding Party. When the first look is happening, go check and make sure the transport vehicle is there!

- Vendor Load in Times (Catering, DJ, Band, Décor, Bakery, Photo Booth). Check in and confirm each vendor.

- Transportation Pick Up Time for Family. Have your assistant at this location to assist with the family getting into the correct vehicle.

- Wedding Party Arrival Time at Venue. Be ready for them to need to drink some water and to use the rest rooms.

- Family Arrival Time at Venue. Help usher the family members to the family photo location.

- Family Photo Time. Make sure the couple has created a list of the photographs they would like. This helps this process go along much more efficiently.

- Guest Transportation Pick Up Time. Have your assistant at this location to assist with the guests getting into the correct vehicle(s). The assistant should ride over with the guests.

- Order of Ceremony Processional. Calmly remind everyone of the order they are walking down the aisle in, hand out tissues if needed, and before you send everyone down the aisle, remind them to walk slow and smile for the camera!

- Ceremony Start Time. Stay close to the ceremony location. Have your assistant stay or you stay. One of you should go check on cocktail hour.

- Cocktail Hour Timing. Make sure everyone is enjoying themselves. If there is a room change from ceremony to reception, make sure all is going smoothly and according to your plan.

- Reception Timing, including Wedding Party introductions, toasts and speeches, blessing, first dance, dances with parents, cake cutting, and thank you by the Couple, as well as any other happenings. Remind everyone 10–15 minutes before they are participating in the evening program when it is their turn!

- Evening Shuttle Start Time. Remind the drivers to be there waiting at the end time of the wedding.

- Last Call. Pack all of the personal items of the couple and get them ready to send off with them or a wedding party or a family member.

- Wedding End Time. Send the happy couple off on their way!

Now, let's go through some tips if the ceremony and reception are at different locations.

- Have a schedule of wedding party members having their hair and make-up done. Each service may take up to 45 minutes per person, per service. Check in with the team and make sure everything is running on time. Kindly remind them of the time you need everyone dressed and out the door.

- Arrival Time of Photographer. Work with the photographer to get any of the detail items ready with them. This includes jewelry, shoes, purse, dress, and any other items the bride would like photographed. Do not get in the way; be there to help them have all of the items they need for these photos.

- Arrival Time of Personal Flowers. Thank them for being on time, and ask if you can assist in the pinning of the boutonnieres and distribution of any of the flowers.

- Dress Time of the Bridesmaids. Remind the ladies 30 minutes before they need to be dressed that they need to be dressed in 30 minutes.

- Dress Time of the Groom and Groomsmen. Remind the guys 30 minutes before they need to be dressed that they need to be dressed in 30 minutes.

- Dress Time of the Bride. Remind the bride before she gets dressed to brush her teeth and that this is her chance to use the restroom before she puts that gown on. It sounds silly, but it is a good idea!

- Arrival Time of Bride's Transportation at the host hotel and the ceremony location.

- Arrival Time of the Groom's Transportation at the host hotel and the ceremony location.

- Transportation Arrival Time for the Guests at the host hotel and the ceremony location. Check on all transportation vehicles. Have the groom leave first, then sneak the bride out and have the vehicles for the guests leave 10 minutes after the bride.

- Order of Ceremony Processional. Calmly remind everyone of the order they are walking down the aisle in, hand out tissues if needed, and before you send everyone down the aisle, remind them to walk slow and smile for the camera!

- Ceremony Start Time. Stay close to the ceremony location.
- Family Photos post ceremony
- Departure time and destination for guest transportation
- Departure time and destination for family transportation
- Departure time and destinations for the wedding party. During the wedding ceremony, remind each driver where they are going next and then the time that they will bring guests over to the reception.
- Vendor Load-in Times (Catering, DJ, Band, Décor, Bakery, Photo Booth). Check in on and confirm each vendor.
- Wedding Party Arrival Time at Venue. Be ready for them to need to drink some water and to use the rest rooms.
- Reception Start Time
- Cocktail Hour Timing. Make sure everyone is enjoying themselves.
- Reception Timing, including wedding party introductions, toasts and speeches, blessing, first dance, dances with parents, cake cutting, and thank you by the Couple, as well as any other happenings. Remind everyone 10–15 minutes before they are participating in the evening program when it is their turn!
- Evening Shuttle Start Time. Remind the drivers to be there waiting at the end time of the wedding.
- Last Call. Pack all of the personal items of the couple and get them ready to send off with them or a wedding party or family member.
- Wedding End Time. Send the happy couple off on their way!

Notes

Notes

Final Wedding Day Survival Tips

- Work together as a team with the other wedding vendors you are coordinating with. If you all pull together, you will be successful.

- Do not tell the Couple if there is anything going wrong. You are there to make things happen correctly for them. Smile and tell them everything is great, and use your team of wedding professionals to correct anything that is not going according to plan.

- Give yourself plenty of time in the timeline and during the day to make things happen. If you think something will take 10 minutes, give yourself 20. This is a joyous day, and not everyone is great at keeping time, nor should they be! Have a buffer so your couple can enjoy themselves.

- Try to keep in contact with key vendors through text messaging so no one can hear if anything is not going according to plan.

- Stay calm and collected. I know there will be stressful moments, but stressing out will not do you any good. You need to think on your feet and be ready to adjust the plan to make the wedding day come together.

- Stay hydrated. It will help you throughout the day and keep you thinking

Well, that is a wrap! Thank you for reading my guide on how to become a successful wedding planner. I know if you have the drive and passion for planning weddings, you are going to be great at it. Just do the work and do it so well that everyone wants to work with you, and you will enjoy a long career in wedding planning. A toast to you on the beginning of your new journey! Cheers!

About Anthony's Career in Wedding & Event Planning

The Early Years

A nthony Navarro has been working professionally in the events field for over 13 years. He began his career working in hotels. While he was attending DePaul University, he acquired a job in the catering sales office as an assistant. Soon after hiring, Anthony was promoted to a full-time sales representative, where his responsibility lied in obtaining corporate and social clients. He was named top sales person in the catering office and had successfully obtained and maintained corporate client connections as well as continued to grow the social event business, including birthday parties, anniversaries, religious celebrations, and weddings. After being successful in the catering department in the hotel, he was transferred to the restaurant inside the hotel to do the same.

An opportunity had arisen for Anthony in a different side of the event planning world at this time with a National Training School for Hospitality Students. Anthony had decided to take the position with the company as the lead instructor of the Chicago location. He was responsible for teaching the curriculum but was also brought on and instructed to teach beyond the base skills. He was teaching the students the modern ways of hospitality and based on his experience and the high expectation that was demanded by most restaurant owners, caterers, and hotel supervisors. Not only did Anthony increase the enrollment for the school but his students gave him high praise and were able to obtain jobs in their desired field with the elevated skill sets. Moreover, this is where Anthony felt the most at home: being in a classroom and helping others accelerate and learn a skill that they wanted to have to begin their careers in hospitality.

After leaving the school for yet another major opportunity to work at one of Chicago's top restaurants and catering companies, Anthony learned yet another accelerated level of service, skill, and expectation. Coming from a family of entrepreneurs, it was not long before he decided to begin a Wedding and Event Planning Company as that is what he is most passionate about.

Building an Event Empire: Liven It Up Events

Anthony has worked hard to build Liven It Up Events to where it is at. He was able to do so with the knowledge and skills he learned throughout his career. What began as a company that planned house parties and retail store events, Liven It Up Events now has a team of seven planners and three co-planners that produce large scale weddings and corporate and social events. In total, every year the company produces an average of 100 events, with budgets ranging from $10,000 to hundreds of thousands of dollars. Liven It Up Events has been awarded as The Best on Yelp!, The Best of The Knot, and the Bride's Choice on Wedding Wire. One of Anthony's weddings produced won the competition reality TV show on TLC, Four Weddings. Anthony was also one of the few wedding planners from Chicago to ever have a wedding featured in Martha Stuart Weddings. And to his surprise, Anthony was named Chicago's Biz Bash Social Event Planner of the Year!

Anthony is also one of the co-founders of the organization STAND UP for Equality, which is an organization for business owners who support marriage equality and one of the creators and co-hosts of the web talk series, "The Wedding Planners."

CPSIA information can be obtained
at www.ICGtesting.com
Printed in the USA
LVOW10s0906130717
541067LV00015B/71/P